IN PARTNERSHIP WITH
IWM

WORLD WAR II

THE DEFINITIVE VISUAL HISTORY

IN WORDS, PHOTOGRAPHS AND RARE ARCHIVE DOCUMENTS

VOLUME II

FROM OPERATION "HUSKY" TO THE JAPANESE SURRENDER, 1943–45

RICHARD OVERY

WELBECK

GENERAL MAP KEY TO SPREAD MAPS

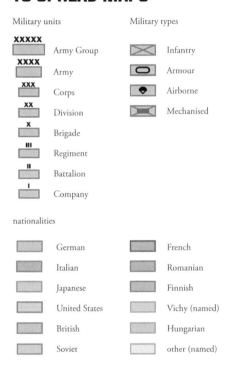

Military units

XXXXX Army Group
XXXX Army
XXX Corps
XX Division
X Brigade
III Regiment
II Battalion
I Company

Military types

Infantry
Armour
Airborne
Mechanised

nationalities

German
Italian
Japanese
United States
British
Soviet

French
Romanian
Finnish
Vichy (named)
Hungarian
other (named)

THIS IS A WELBECK BOOK
Design and map copyright © Welbeck Non-fiction Limited 2020
Text copyright © Richard Overy 2008, 2009, 2020
Imperial War Museum photographs and memorabilia
© Imperial War Museum

This edition published in 2020 by Welbeck
An imprint of the Welbeck Publishing Group
20 Mortimer Street
London
W1T 3JW

Originally published in four volumes by Carlton Books in 2008–2009 as *The Second World War Experience: Blitzkrieg 1939–41*; *Axis Ascendant 1941–42*; *Turning of the Tide 1942–43*; *The Struggle for Victory 1944–45*.
This edition contains a selection of material from *Turning of the Tide 1942–43* and *The Struggle for Victory 1944–45*.

Printed in Dubai

A CIP catalogue for this book is available from the British Library

ISBN: 978 0 233 00621 5

Cover photographs
Front: Imperial War Museums, London (A 023997)
Back: Imaperial War Museums, London (NY 006082)

CONTENTS

INTRODUCTION

The year 1943 was the turning point of the war in all the major theatres across the globe. What had begun as a series of wars to establish new empires for Japan, Italy and Germany merged by 1943 into a single vast conflict, bound together by the global reach of the United States whose vast industrial resources, raw materials and foodstuffs were sending vital assistance to the Soviet Union in its struggle with the European Axis powers, to Britain as it fought wars in the Mediterranean and southern Asia, and to China, locked after six years of attrition warfare in a stalemate against Japan.

OPPOSITE Soviet T-34/85 tanks on the road towards Königsberg in late January/early February 1945. To save on vehicles and fuel, Soviet infantry assigned to armoured formations travelled on top of the tanks. The mixed-arm units introduced gradually from 1943 gave the Red Army the flexibility and fighting power enjoyed earlier by Germany's Panzer divisions.

American economic might was a critical factor in turning the tide against the aggressors. In January 1943, President Roosevelt announced at the Casablanca conference with Churchill that the Allied powers would accept nothing less than unconditional surrender. This was something the Axis leaders could never agree to. From 1943 until their utter defeat in 1945 they tried to avoid the inevitable. The toughest fighting of the war took place in the last two years.

The long retreat of the Axis powers began after German and Italian defeat in Tunisia in May 1943, Soviet victory at the Battle of Kursk in July that year, and the American capture of the island of Guadalcanal in the south Pacific after six months of gruelling combat. After that, long wars of attrition set in in the Pacific, in the conquest of Italy, in the drive from Kursk to the borders of Germany, and the Western Allies' combination of strategic bombing and the invasion of France. In every case the Allies had a long learning curve to become as effective at fighting as Japan had been in 1941–2 and Germany since the invasion of Poland in September 1939. Large resources were important, but they had to be used on the battlefield in ways to ensure victory. The Red army and air force began to imitate German practice with large mechanised forces and central control of air fleets; the Americans learned how to turn amphibious warfare doctrine into amphibious practice, culminating in the massive assaults on Iwo Jima and Okinawa. The British Commonwealth forces learned, too, how to use tanks and tactical air forces more productively and in tandem. German and Japanese forces also upgraded technology and observed their enemies' battlefield performance closely, but once they were faced with the overwhelming resources of Allies who had learned enough to use them well, the final outcome was not in doubt.

The first to crumble was Italy. Benito Mussolini was overthrown and the new Italian government sued for peace in September 1943. Mussolini retreated north with his German allies and set up a puppet Fascist regime, the Italian Social Republic, which continued to fight the Allies until the end of the war. Japan suffered defeat after defeat in the south and central Pacific, but so wide was the new Japanese empire, that it took years to clear a way across the islands to retake the Philippines and to approach the Japanese home islands. Japan's forces fought literally with suicidal intent. Almost no one was taken captive. In Europe, the Soviet forces drove the Germans back step by step, but even in retreat German forces fought with determination and skill. In Italy, the geography of mountains and river valleys running up the peninsula, held up Allied forces for eighteen months of costly combat. In France, the Germans expected an invasion and when it came made strenuous efforts to contain it, but as in the East, numbers wore them down and the loss of air power at the fighting front, due to the attrition of fighter forces combating the bombing campaign, gave the Allies a vital edge.

Hitler refused to surrender and shot himself in April 1945 as Soviet soldiers closed in on his bunker in Berlin; Japanese military leaders saw surrender as morally unacceptable and preferred to die until two atomic bombs and the Soviet conquest of Manchuria in August 1945 persuaded Emperor Hirohito that the time had come to give up. Even before the end of the war, the Allied powers sought to construct a new world order. The United Nations came into being in May 1945 as the German war ended. Hopes for peace were high, but the division of Europe and Korea between Western and Soviet influence sowed the seeds of the Cold War and the wars in Korea and Vietnam. The main achievement in 1945 was to end the age of territorial imperialism. The German, Japanese and Italian empires disappeared overnight; the British, French, Dutch and Belgian empires all unravelled in the twenty years that followed.

RICHARD OVERY, SEPTEMBER 2019

OPERATION "HUSKY": INVASION OF SICILY

It was agreed at the Casablanca Conference that the invasion of Sicily would follow the defeat of the Axis in North Africa. Planning began in the spring for Operation "Husky", which was assigned to General Alexander's 15th Army Group, made up of Montgomery's 8th Army and Patton's 1st US Armored Corps (renamed 7th US Army for the invasion). The object was to land in force on the southern and southeastern coast and to sweep up the island quickly enough to prevent Axis forces from escaping to the mainland. The date was set for 10 July 1943.

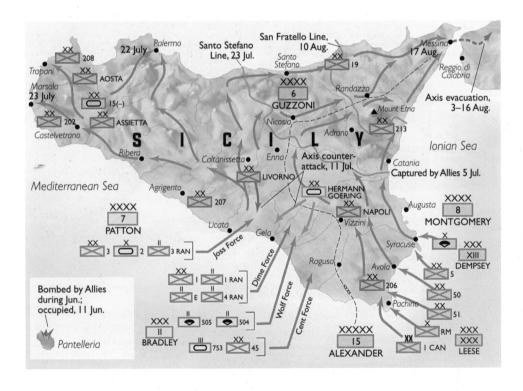

12 JULY 1943
Red Army begins Operation "Kutuzov" against the German-held city of Orel following the end of "Zitadelle".

17 JULY 1943
Following Allied deceptive measures, Hitler orders reinforcements to go to Greece to resist an expected Allied invasion of the region.

1 AUGUST 1943
Japan declares Burma to be an independent state, though under close Japanese supervision.

5 AUGUST 1943
US forces complete the capture of New Georgia in the Solomons.

12 AUGUST 1943
A force of over 600 RAF bombers attacks the major Italian industrial centre of Milan.

In order to render the ambitious amphibious operation more secure – it was second in size only to the later invasion of France – a risky deception plan was mounted codenamed Operation "Mincemeat" which involved leaving a dead body dressed in the uniform of a Royal Marines major off the Spanish coast with false Allied plans concealed in a briefcase. The body was handed to the British consul, but the briefcase was kept by the Spanish authorities and its contents revealed to the German consul. The fake plan described an Allied operation against Greece with Sicily as a diversion. The ruse worked perfectly and German forces were strengthened in Greece and Sardinia, but not in Sicily.

Air power was to play an important part in the invasion. In June, an Italian garrison on the island of Pantelleria, lying on the route from North Africa to Sicily, was so pulverized by bombing that the garrison surrendered without an invasion. Aircraft neutralized any threat from Axis air forces

during the invasion. On 9 July, the operation began with American and British paratroop landings to secure vital bridges and communications. Strong winds produced a disaster, with 200 British paratroopers drowning in the sea. Out of 2,781 US paratroops, only 200 arrived at the objective near the Sicilian port of Licata. During the night of 9–10 July, a flotilla of 2,590 ships and landing craft approached Sicily, carrying 180,000 men. They were faced by approximately 50,000 German and 270,000 Italian troops, but it was expected that most Italians would have little stomach for the battle.

OPPOSITE Operation "Husky", 10 July–17 August 1943

ABOVE An aerial view of the island of Pantelleria during a heavy Allied air bombardment in June 1943. The island was on the route to Sicily and the garrison had to be eliminated before the landings on Sicily could begin.

GENERAL MILES DEMPSEY
(1896–1969)

Dempsey was one of Montgomery's most successful 8th Army generals. He served with the Royal Berkshire Regiment in the First World War, and continued to do so in the interwar years. He fought in France in 1940, and as a lieutenant general was sent to command the 13th Corps of the 8th Army, which he led in North Africa, Sicily and Italy. He commanded the 2nd Army in the Normandy invasion and ended the war accepting the surrender of Hamburg in 1945. He became Commander-in-Chief Allied Land Forces in Southeast Asia, and was Commander-in-Chief in the Middle East in 1946–47 during the crisis in Palestine. He retired from the army in July 1947 and was Commander-in-Chief of UK Land Forces Designate from 1951 to 1956.

GENERAL GEORGE S. PATTON

(1885–1945)

One of the most controversial but successful of American generals during the Second World War, Patton joined the US cavalry in 1909, fought in Mexico in 1916 and in France in 1917–18, first on the staff of the US commander General Pershing, then in command of a tank brigade. In January 1942, he took command of the 1st Armored Corps. He commanded the western task force which landed at Casablanca in November 1942, and commanded the 2nd US Army Corps in Tunisia in March and April 1943, before being recalled to plan the invasion of Sicily. His public persona was flamboyant, aggressive and coarse, and he famously flaunted a pair of ivory-handled pistols, but he was also a scrupulous and hardworking commander. He made morale a high priority, but when he assaulted and abused two combat-weary soldiers in the Sicilian campaign to get them to carry on fighting, the incident almost ended his career. He was recalled to command the 3rd US Army in the Normandy invasion, and his aggression and operational awareness made him an outstanding armoured commander. He was made a four-star general in April 1945, but died in a car accident eight months later.

British forces landed without difficulty on the beaches at Avola and Pachino, and US forces faced serious opposition only at Gela, where the Hermann Göring Division was stationed. Within five days, Allied forces had pushed inland to a line from Agrigento to the Gulf of Catania. Progress proved slow in mountainous terrain, which gave every advantage to the defender against an armoured attack. Patton was supposed to protect the flank of the 8th Army as it struck north to Messina and northwest to the central Sicilian city of Enna, but the collapse of Italian resistance against his aggressive armoured drive persuaded him that the whole of the west of the island could fall quickly into Allied hands. This was one of many arguments that continued to sour Anglo-American co-operation. Alexander reluctantly agreed, and Patton's units reached Palermo on 22 July.

Montgomery's progress proved frustratingly slow and Catania was taken only on 5 August. By this time, Alexander had ordered Patton's forces to swing east towards Messina to assist the 1st Canadian Division as it looped west of Mount Etna, on a trajectory initially assigned to the American zone. In the midst of the final push towards Messina, the Italian dictator, Benito Mussolini, was overthrown on 25 July 1943. Hitler, who had insisted on no withdrawal, was compelled to order an evacuation across the Straits of Messina. The Italian army under General Alfredo Guzzoni saw little point in continued resistance. By the time Allied forces converged on Messina, over 100,000 Italian and German forces had successfully been removed, without any serious air or naval action by the Allies. Patton arrived in the centre of Messina two hours before the British on 17 August, but the trap had failed to be sprung and one-third of Axis forces escaped. The campaign cost the Allies 25,000 casualties, but approximately 115,000 Italian soldiers surrendered in the course of the campaign, no longer willing to fight for a cause that had collapsed.

OPPOSITE A defaced portrait of Mussolini hangs on a lamppost in northern Sicily on the road from Messina to the coast, with German and Italian road signs beneath it. Mussolini fell from power on 25 July.

OPERATION "HUSKY"

The final plan for Operation "Husky", drawn up on 4–5 June 1943 following the defeat of Axis forces in Tunisia in May. Eisenhower remained the overall Commander-in-Chief while the British general, Harold Alexander, took command of forces in the field.

From: AFHQ in North Africa
to: WAR

No. W 2005, June 4, 1943.

To AGWAR. Signed Eisenhower. HUSKY BIGOT. Cite FHGCT. Of 3 parts. Part 1.

1. After preparatory action to gain air supremacy, basis of final HUSKY plan, outlined below for your information, is predawn seaborn assaults, assisted by airborne landings, to seize Siracusa, Licata, and airfields in SE Sicily, in order establish firm base for operations against Augusta, Catania, and airfields Gerbini area.

2. Outline Task Force plans, based on force 141 directive, are:
    A. Twelfth Army's assault between Siracusa and Pozallo to capture Siracusa Port and Pachino Airfield. After gaining touch force 343 east of Comiso to effect rapid capture Augusta, Catania and airfields Gerbini. Thirty Corps, after capturing Pachino Airfield and town, has 2nd and 3rd objectives Road Avola-Pozallo and line Palazzolo-Ragusa respectively, gaining touch force 343 east of Comiso. Fifty one Div advances on right, Canadians left. Thirteen Corps, eventually including Seventy Eight Div, after relief of Fifty Div west of Avola by Thirty Corps, advances on Augusta, Catania and Gerbini, Fifty Div first seizing high ground west of Augusta.

    B. Force 343. Assault between Sampieri and Licata to capture by dark D plus 2 Licata port and airfields. Ponte Olivo, Biscari and Comiso. Beachhead to be extended to line Palma De Montechiaro-Compobello-Mazzarino-Grammichel, including high ground Piazza Amerina Aidone. After gaining touch 12th Army, to protect captured port and airfields and guard left flank 12th Army against enemy reserves.

3. Allotment of troops to assault is:
    A. 12th Army. D day assaults. Ship to Shore EX Mideast, Avola North Beach 44, Five Div, 15 Bde right to seize Cassibile 17 Bde left eventually passing north through 15 Bde. Avola South Beaches 47 and 48, 50th Div, 151 Bde assaulting, objective high ground west Avola. Pachino East Beaches 51 and 52, 231 Bde Gp, to protect north flank 30th Corps and join up with Canadians. Shore to shore EX Tunisia and Malta, Pachino South, 51st Div assaults to Bns west 1 Bn east of Beach 56 to seize beach from rear, secure high ground south of Pachino Airfield and subsequently capture Pachino airfield and subsequently capture Pachino town. Ship to shore EX UK, Pachino West Beach 57, 1 Canadian Div and 1 Tank Bn, 2 Bde assault to capture Pachino airfield and marshes west Pachino to protect left flank 30th Corps. Reserve to be called forward as expedient shore to shore EX Sousse/Sfax 78th Div and Canadian Tank Bde less 1 Bn. Nomination follow up division not firm; Force 141 anxious use 8th Army Div, but 46th Div being prepared in case no 8th Army Div available. Avola assaults 13th Corps. Pachino assaults 30th Corps.

End Part 1. Part 2 follows.

ACTION: OPD   SECRET   "No Sig

CM-IN-2736   (5 Jun 43)   0240Z   ems   SECURITY

From: AFHQ North Africa
To: WAR
No: W 2004, June 4, 1943.

Two parts - Part 1 of 3 parts - Part 2
To AGWAR. Signed Eisenhower. HUSKY BIGOT. Cite FHGCT.

3. B. Force 343, D day assaults. Pozallo, 45 Div mainly ship to shore EX Oran, and Gela, 1 Div less 1 RCT mainly ship to shore EX Algiers, make corps assault beaches 59 to 69 to capture Ponte Olivo airfield daylight D plus 1, airfields Comiso and Biscari daylight and dark respectively D plus 2. Then extend beachhead and gain touch 3 Div. JOSS)(Licata Beaches 70 to 74, 3 Div and 1 Armd CC shore to shore ES Tunis/Bizerte, to capture Licata port and airfield by dark D day. Floating reserve available on call, 2 Armd Div less 1 Armd CC and 1 RCT 1 Div, ship to shore and shore to shore EX North Africa follow up 9 Div. Pozallo and Gela assaults 2 Corps.

4. Employment of airborne troops. First and 82nd Airborne Divs allotted for support 12th Army and 343rd respectively. Two thirds available troop carrying aircraft allotted force 343 and one third 12th Army.

    A. Approximately 1 BDE Gp, 1st Airborne Div, gliders and paratroops, land 2300 hours D minus 1 west of Siracusa to assist 5 Div by seizing key bridges and points on outskirts town. Concurrently Siracusa to be bombed and diversion created west of Catania. Similar airborne operations, dependent on progress made, will assist 50 Div west of Augusta night D Day/ D plus 1 and 13 Corps during subsequent advance to Catania.

    B. Paratroops 82nd Airborne Div in support 2nd Corps, details not yet final. Div less paratroops in force reserve on call from H hour.

5. Subsequent operations. After initial assaults, operations will be designed to establish force 141 on line Catania-Licata, with view to final operations for reduction of Sicily.

6. Maintenance will follow generally the principles given in paragraphs 8 to 15 of 3rd outline maintenance project dated 15th April.

End of part 2. Part 3 and last follows.

From: AFHQ North Africa
To : WAR
No. : W 2006, June 4, 1943.

Of 3 parts, Part 3 and last. To AGWAR. Signed Eisenhower.
HUSKY BIGOT. Cite FHGCT

7. Force EX UK brings 24 days maintenance plus 10 days reserve.
British Force EX NA, 51 Div brings 21 days maintenance plus 10 days reserve in assault and subsequent Ferry Service. Seventy-eight Div
brings 21 days maintenance plus 10 days reserve. Forces EX Mideast
bring 7 days maintenance in MW 1 assault convoy. Follow up MW 2
carries 12 days maintenance requirements for forces EX Mideast landed
in assault and 1st follow up plus 8 days reserve for British Force
eventually to be assembled in Sicily. Subsequent maintenance all
British Forces up to D plus 42 convoy exclusive will be EX Mideast.
D plus 42 and subsequent convoys from west planned by Mideast until
Hq Force 141 and Freedom assume administrative control, but certain
items of Eastern Group Supply will emanate from Mideast. Responsibility for POL and source of supply after D plus 42 still under
discussion.

8. US maintenance. Forty-five Div EX US brings 21 days
maintenance for Pozallo, Gela EX NA brings 7 days with assault.
Each follow up brings 7 days maintenance plus 7 days for troops
previously landed. JOSS EX NA maintained by landing craft and
Coaster Ferry Service.

9. Reinforcements 12 Army. First RFTS 5 and 50 Divs from
Mideast on planned convoy program. First RFTS for PMNS mounted NA
from NA on planned program. All subsequent RFTS held base depots
NA and fed into Adv RFTS units in Sicily. Recovered personnel EX
hospitals Tripoli to base depots NA. Canadian RFTS to Base Depots NA
and forward with British RFTS to own units.

10. Replacements 343. Two Bns held forward for early move to
Sicily. Further replacements Bns held in base section NA.

11. Medical. Initial evacuation 12th Army. Will be from
beaches by hospital ships and carriers Tripoli and in the case of
1 CDN Div to Sousse. In addition lightly wounded may be evacuated
from 51 Div by LSTs to Sousse-Sfax. Minor cases with a hospital
expectancy of less than 7 days will be retained in Sicily. Initial
evacuation force 343 by hospital ships and combat loaders to Bizerte
and Tunis. Malta will not be used for general evacuation but can
accept up to 400 casualties a day brought in ships and craft calling
there. A proportion of General Hospitals will be landed as soon as
possible after ports are open. Evacuation will be from ports as soon
as these are open, to Philippeville, Tripoli and Ocean Atlantic. Cases
with a hospital expectancy of less than 3 months to Mideast, except

for CDN Div cases with a hospital expectancy of more than 3 months
to NA for UK. Subsequent to this build up of General Hospitals in
Sicily, cases with a hospital expectancy of less than 42 days will
be retained in Sicily. Otherwise evacuation will be as above. End
of Part 3.

CM-IN-2795 (5 June 43)

3 SEPTEMBER–1 OCTOBER 1943

ITALY: INVASION AND SURRENDER

The decision to invade Italy after the conquest of Sicily in August 1943 was accelerated by the fall of Mussolini's regime on 25 July. The Allies hoped to be able to capitalize on the change in government to take Italy out of the war before the Germans could reinforce the peninsula adequately. Negotiations with the new regime of Marshal Badoglio were slow to produce a result. On 3 September the Italian armistice was signed at Cassibile, but by that point the Germans had succeeded in strengthening their forces in Italy from six to 18 divisions. It was essential for German strategy that the Allies should be kept as far south as possible, to avoid the establishment of airfields for the bombing of southern Germany and to make it impossible to use Italy as a military roadway into German-occupied Europe.

By the time the armistice was formally announced on 8 September, the Allies had already begun to move onto the Italian mainland. The plan was to land substantial forces in the Gulf of Salerno, south of Naples, and then to move northwards rapidly to take Naples and Rome and south to take over the Italian "heel and toe". Lieutenant General Mark Clark was put in command of the US 5th Army, consisting of the US 6th Corps and the British 10th Corps, which would land on either side of the River Sele which flowed into the gulf. Before this operation, Montgomery took part of the 8th Army across the Straits of Messina to land unopposed on the morning of 3 September, shortly before the armistice came into effect. The 8th Army then began to push up through Calabria with the eventual aim of meeting up with the forces sent ashore at Salerno.

The situation in Italy was chaotic following the declaration of the armistice; Badoglio, the king and the General Staff fled south to join

17–24 AUGUST 1943

Allied Quadrant Conference in Quebec confirms Normandy operation and Anglo-American co-operation over use of an atomic bomb.

7 SEPTEMBER 1943

Corsicans begin uprising against Axis occupation.

12 SEPTEMBER 1943

Mussolini is freed from prison by an SS glider unit.

19 SEPTEMBER 1943

German forces abandon the Italian island of Sardinia.

22 SEPTEMBER 1943

First bridgeheads made across the Dnieper River by the Red Army in pursuit of retreating Axis forces.

25 SEPTEMBER 1943

Smolensk recaptured by Western Army Group under General Sokolovsky.

4 OCTOBER 1943

Corsica is liberated from Axis occupation.

GENERAL MARK CLARK
(1896–1984)

One of the best-known American generals in the Second World War, Clark rose from the rank of major in the 1930s to become, by mid-1942, Chief-of-Staff of US Army Ground Forces with the strong backing of his mentor, General George Marshall. In October 1942, he was made deputy Commander-in-Chief of Allied forces in North Africa, and went on to lead the US 5th Army for the invasion of Italy in September 1943 as the youngest lieutenant general in the army. Though he was often criticized for his handling of operations in Italy, including the decision to bombard the historic monastery at Monte Cassino, he became Commander-in-Chief of all Allied ground forces in Italy in December 1944 and by the end of the war was Commander of all Allied forces in Italy. In 1949, he became Chief of Army Field Forces and commanded the United Nations forces in the Korean War, signing the ceasefire with North Korea in 1953.

British troops and vehicles of the 8th Army's 46th Division unload on the beach at Salerno, 9 September 1943. After meeting light resistance at first, the bridgehead came under heavy attack.

the Allies, leaving no orders for the large Italian army. German forces immediately disarmed Italian soldiers, but in some cases they resisted, only to be brutally treated and shot out of hand. Some 650,000 Italian soldiers were sent as POWs to Germany, where they became forced labourers. The Italian fleet fled to Malta, but was hit by the German air force with new remote-controlled bombs and the battleship *Roma* was sunk. The country was divided in two, the far south governed by Badoglio together with the

Allies, the north by a new Fascist Italian Social Republic, based in the town of Salò on the shores of Lake Garda, with Mussolini as its nominal leader but the German authorities under Field Marshal Kesselring the real rulers.

On 9 September, Clark's task force sailed for Salerno, already aware that the landing would be strongly resisted by the German occupiers. A fleet of 627 ships arrived off the coast and the naval vessels subjected the coastal area to a fierce bombardment. The British forces under Lieutenant

German anti-tank unit in combat with Allied forces on the perimeter around the Salerno bridgehead. German forces almost succeeded in forcing the Allies to evacuate.

General McCreery landed to the north of the Gulf of Salerno and the Americans under Major General Dawley in the south; although small bridgeheads were secured, shortages of air support and the stiff resistance of the Panzer divisions assigned to the German defence led to a dangerous situation by 12 September, as General von Vietinghoff's growing force began a powerful counter-offensive.

The Allies made tentative plans for evacuation, but the 82nd US Airborne Division was dropped into the danger zone, while aircraft and extra naval vessels were drafted in to bombard the enemy, and by 16 September German forces began to pull back. By 20 September, the rest of the 8th Army, making its way against much lighter opposition from Taranto and Bari, established firm contact with the Salerno beachhead. The German force pulled back to a prepared line north of Naples, and the port was occupied by Allied forces on 1 October. The scene was now set for a long and bitter campaign through difficult mountain country along the whole length of the Italian peninsula.

COLONEL GENERAL HEINRICH VON VIETINGHOFF (1887–1952)

A career soldier from an aristocratic military family, von Vietinghoff served in the First World War as a junior officer on the General Staff, and by 1936 was a major general in command of a Panzer corps. In August 1943, he was sent to command the 10th Army in Italy, which he did until January 1945, when he was posted briefly as commander of the army group defending Courland against the Red Army. He acted as deputy for Kesselring as Commander-in-Chief Southwest from October 1944 to January 1945, and was then made full Commander-in-Chief from 15 March 1945 until 29 April, when he surrendered his forces to the Allies. After the war, he was one of a group of experts recruited by Chancellor Adenauer who recommended German inclusion in a Western European defence system.

EIGHTH ARMY NEWS

Friday, 3 SEPTEMBER, 1943   No 41. Vol. 2   SICILY

WE INVADE ITALY

BOMBERS AND NAVAL GUNS BLAST GERMAN BATTERIES

Eighth Army has invaded the Mainland of Italy. Our soldiers landed on the beaches between Gallico and San Giovanni at 4.30 this morning, 3rd September. Early reports indicate that the operation is meeting with entire success. Our forces have reached the outskirts of Reggio.

The attack began with a heavy artillery barrage. There was little opposition, and Italians on the beaches and in the hills appeared with white flags. What opposition there is comes from German medium artillery sited in the hills.

Enemy batteries are being dealt with by our land forces, air striking force, and the Royal Navy. When forward observation officers with the army require naval shelling they signal to our monitors and cruisers who, in the words of a naval spokesman, « deal with any of the enemy who are making a nuisance of themselves ».

Here is the full text of the communique issued by Allied HQ.

« British and Canadian troops of the Eighth Army supported by Allied sea and air power, attacked across the Straits of Messina early today and landed on the mainland of Italy.

« Allied forces under the command of General Eisenhower have continued their advance. »

Rome radio made no mention of the landing in its 9 o'clock broadcast.

Fighting is expected to be severe owing to the mountainous nature of the country and bad communications.

The main physical feature of the Italian mainland opposite the Straits of Messina is a backbone of mountains among which towers Monte Alto, nearly 6,000 feet high. Monte Alto, with its outrunners, dominates the approaches to Calabria, Italy's southernmost province. The railways

Eighth Army marches on. Alamein to Tunis — Tunis to Sicily. And now the next may be Rome.

to the north must traverse the narrow coastal strip on either side of this mountain backbone.

Air Offensive

Our invasion was preceded by a great air offensive.

Allied bombers flew on thirty-one missions, and despite heavy cloud which tended to obscure their objectives, twenty-three of these missions found their targets.

The enemy airfield at Crotone, one of the Germans' main forward landing bases, was viciously attacked.

When enemy artillery was reported in the toe outside our artillery range, bombers smashed home at it.

Two areas where the enemy might have assembled forces for counter-attack were also plastered.

We suffered no losses in bombers. In fact not one single mission was molested.

The enemy attempted to sneak in an attack on Augusta harbour. In the first of these attempts he used fifteen

Over the Channel

As part of the plan to give the extended German Air Force no respite, Allied aircraft were out in force over the Channel yesterday.

Streams of Bostons, Mitchells, Marauders and Fortresses, with Spitfire and Hurricane escorts, swept out at dusk yesterday to bomb German airfields in France, a power station, railway junctions and other targets.

Earlier in the day lock gates on an important Dutch canal were bombed. Hits were scored on three of the locks.

We lost two bombers and two fighters against the enemy's loss of four machines.

GERMANS SPEED RETREAT

Red Army Gains Vital Railpoints

With the great Russian summer offensive gaining in momentum, the German retreat in some sectors is showing signs of getting out of hand. Moscow makes this statement in a communique announcing more from east of Smolensk to the Sea of spectacular successes on the vast front Azov.

These successes include the capture of Sumi, about 90 miles N.W. of Kharkov, and a vital junction in the secondary railway lines remaining in German hands since the loss of the Moscow-Kharkov line; the cutting of the railway linking Bryansk, at the northern end of the front, with the Ukraine and with Kiev, and the capture of Lisichansk, Voroshilovsk and several other towns on the south bank of the Donetz River.

From north to south the position is now as follows:

More Towns Fall

The Russians have made more progress in their drive on Smolensk. Yesterday they were reported 45 miles east of the city. One hundred more places have fallen into Russian hands.

At Yelnya on this front the Germans have launched heavy counter attacks.

Railway Cut

On the Bryansk front, 140 miles to the south-east, the Red Army has made spectacular progress. After beating off German counter-attacks North, West and south-west of Sevsk, the Russians cut the railway linking Bryansk with Kiev.

The capture of Sumi, halfway between Kharkov and the Bryansk-Kiev railway is announced in a special Order of the Day by Marshal Stalin. Last night 120 of Moscow's big guns fired 12 salvos to celebrate this important gain, which will simplify considerably the Red Army's communication problems.

In the plains, West and South of Kharkov, Soviet troops have advanced again and captured another strongpoint South of the city.

It is in the Donetz Basin however that the Russians are making the swiftest progress. Here the German retreat shows signs of becoming a rout and they are suffering heavy losses in their flight.

Nearing Stalino

The Red Army is systematically clearing the Germans from the Lower Don basin and the capture of several more towns on the south bank of the Donetz has brought them appreciably nearer to Stalino, key to the whole German defences in this area. The Russians are also pushing the enemy along the northern shores of the sea of Azov and were last night reported only 25 miles from Mariupol, the next important town west of Taganrog.

The Russian air force has complete mastery of the skies and by its repeated bombings of concentration points behind the enemy lines is doing much to hinder the launching of effective counter-attacks.

Jobs Promised

«Yes, sir», was the reply of Mr. Bevin, Minister of Labour when asked by Sir Ian Fraser (Con., Lonsdale) in the Commons if he could give an assurance that everything possible will be done to see that fighting men who return from the war particularly from distant theatres will have a job to come back to.

THE FIRST TO LAND

The following message from General Montgomery has been read to Eighth Army:—

1. Having captured SICILY as our first slice of the Italian home country, the time has now come to carry the battle on to the mainland of Italy.

2. To the Eighth Army has been given the great honour of being the first troops of the Allied Armies to land on the mainland of the continent of Europe.

We will prove ourselves worthy of this honour.

3. I want to tell all of you, soldiers of the Eighth Army, that I have complete confidence in the successful outcome of the operations we are now going to carry out.

We have a good plan, and air support on a greater scale than we have ever had before.

There can only be one end to this next battle, and that is: ANOTHER SUCCESS.

4. Forward to Victory!

Let us knock ITALY out of the war!

5. Good luck. And God Bless you all.

200 TONS ON JAPS

Allied bombers have given Japanese installations in New Guinea one of the heaviest poundings of the war.

More than 200 tons of bombs were unloaded on Madang. Fuel and ammunition dumps were blown up. At least 50 fires were counted by our pilots.

During the raid the Allied pilots destroyed the only aircraft on the runway at Madang.

Lae and Salamaua were also raided.

When the Japanese attempted to raid Allied installations on Vela la Vela in the Solomons, five of their aircraft were shot down by fighters and four others by AA fire.

"DO IT AGAIN"

« Do it again» shouted an Australian commando, stepping into the open as a sniper's bullet narrowly missed him.

The sniper obliged revealed his position and the Australian drew his pistol and shot him dead.

This is one of the stories told by an American now in Australia, who has served with the Australian Commandos in New Guinea.

Another illustration of commando daring is his story of a party of Australians who came upon a party of Japs preparing their dinner in the jungle.

The Aussies waited until the meal was cooked, then sailed in, killed the eight hungry Japs and ate the meal themselves.

Seven Mile Fall

London.

Early this week it was announced that a German plane flying at a height of 7 miles up had been shot down by a British AA battery.

Today it is officially stated that the plane was a Messerschmidt 109 Germany's latest high flying plane, made at the Wiener Neustadt factory recently battered by American Liberators.

It came over Britain to make photographic reconnaissance and was shepherded over the Channel by two other planes.

[Reuter]

While police, crofters shepherds and hill villagers searched the lonely Glencoe region in Scotland for 2-year-old Cyril Watkins of London, who had been missing for a week, letter arrived at his home at Cricklewood stating that he had gained the degree of B.Sc.

29 JUNE 1943–APRIL 1944

OPERATION "CARTWHEEL": WAR FOR NEW GUINEA

Following the defeat of the Japanese on Guadalcanal in February 1943, the Japanese naval and military leaders planned to strengthen their presence on New Guinea and to hold a defensive line from there through the northern Solomons to the Gilbert and Marshall islands. During the first three months of 1943, Lieutenant General Hatazo Adachi's 18th Army was transferred to the eastern coast of New Guinea and a large air component, the 4th Air Army, was based at Wewak, far enough from the American and Australian air forces in the southern tip of the island to avoid direct attack. The object was to move back down the island to capture Port Moresby, the target for Japanese ambitions a year before.

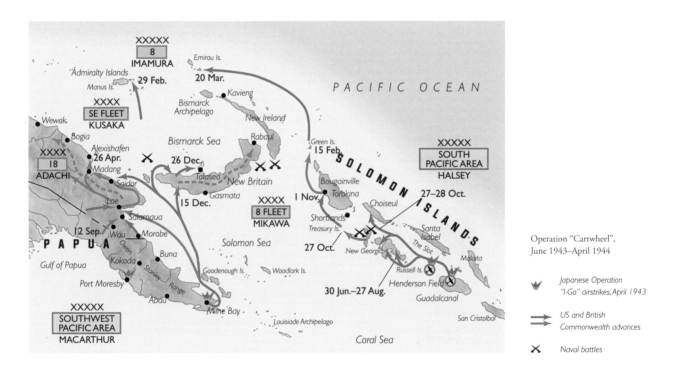

Operation "Cartwheel",
June 1943–April 1944

⛉ Japanese Operation
"I-Go" airstrikes, April 1943

⇒ US and British
Commonwealth advances

✕ Naval battles

General MacArthur planned to consolidate the victory at Guadalcanal, which had demonstrated the growing superiority of American naval power in the southwest Pacific, by launching a major operation, codenamed "Cartwheel", against the main Japanese base at Rabaul on New Britain and the Japanese forces in northern New Guinea. On New Guinea itself an Australian army group, the New Guinea Force, with five Australian divisions and one American, was assigned to attack the Japanese based at Lae and Salamaua. The all-American Alamo Force, backed by a powerful naval and air component, was to neutralize Rabaul and attack New Britain and the Admiralty Islands, further to the north.

The Japanese attacked first in an attempt to seize the Allied airstrip at Wau but they were beaten off in bitter fighting. Then, on 29 June, the Allied attack began on the Japanese bases at Lae and Salamaua. To speed up the advance, Lieutenant General Kenney's US 5th Air Force

5 JULY 1943

Start of Operation "Zitadelle" for the capture of the Kursk salient.

8 SEPTEMBER 1943

Announcement of the Italian surrender prompts German occupation of most of mainland Italy.

6 NOVEMBER 1943

Ukrainian capital Kiev recaptured by the Red Army.

22 JANUARY 1944

Anglo-American force lands on the Italian coast at Anzio to speed up the Allied drive towards Rome.

20 FEBRUARY 1944

RAF Bomber Command and US 8th Air Force begin the "Big Week" attack on German aircraft production.

15 MARCH 1944

Start of Japanese U-Go offensive on the Imphal Plain.

10 APRIL 1944

The Red Army captures Odessa with Malinowski's 3rd Ukrainian Army Group.

built a secret airfield closer to the Japanese air base at Wewak from which he launched two devastating attacks on 17 and 18 August, leaving the Japanese with just 38 serviceable aircraft. The Japanese army defended to the death, and not until 16 September did the Australians overrun Lae and Salamaua, and another three months were needed before the whole of the Huon Peninsula was in Allied hands.

While this first campaign was completed, US forces landed on western New Britain on 15 December. The previous month, strong carrier forces

ABOVE A Beaufort Bomber of No. 8 Squadron Royal Australian Air Force above the shoreline during a bombing attack on Wewak, the site of the largest Japanese airbase on mainland New Guinea.

RIGHT A Japanese national flag, given to Japanese soldiers by friends and family and carried to encourage personal good luck and patriotic virtue. They were inscribed with messages of good fortune and slogans of victory and honour to the emperor.

THE BATTLE OF THE BISMARCK SEA

On 28 February 1943, 7,000 men of the Japanese 51st Division embarked in eight transport vessels at the main Japanese base at Rabaul in the northern Solomon Islands, bound for northern New Guinea. They were escorted by eight destroyers. American forces had been warned in advance of the convoy through Pacific ULTRA intelligence and on 2 March began a series of attacks by day and night as the boats crossed the Bismarck Sea. All the transport vessels were sunk and four of the destroyers, with the loss of c. 3,000 of the division. The Japanese commander in New Guinea, Lieutenant General Hatazo Adachi, was among the 950 survivors to reach the Japanese base at Lae.

United States troops rush ashore during the landing at Saidor on the northern coast of New Guinea, 2 January 1944. This was part of the coast-hopping operations designed to outflank the Japanese defenders during Operation "Cartwheel".

Australian soldiers crossing the Faria River in New Guinea on their way back to base. Australian forces played a major part in the fight against the Japanese on the island.

had neutralized any threat from the Japanese base at Rabaul, while the main concentration of the Japanese fleet, at the island of Truk in the Carolines group further north, was too weak to contest every avenue of American advance. After landings in the Admiralty Islands between 29 February and 20 March 1944, the American Fast Carrier Force commanded by Vice Admiral Marc Mitscher swung round to mount operations on the northern coast of New Guinea far behind Adachi's retreating 18th Army, cutting off his avenue of escape. Strong forces were landed at Hollandia and Aitape on 22 April. Adachi ordered his force to attack the US perimeter in July 1944, but was beaten back. He retreated with what was left of his force into the high mountains inland, and played no further part in the war.

Operation "Cartwheel" confirmed that the balance of power had swung firmly in favour of the Allies in the southwest Pacific. Although the Japanese had held the long frontier of their conquered Pacific empire for two years, it was only because fighting in the tough tropical conditions of the region was a slow process, while Japanese forces resisted with almost complete disregard for their losses and in spite of debilitating diseases and persistent hunger. The refusal to give up lent the fighting a brutal character which Allied forces did not encounter in the Mediterranean or Western Europe.

LIEUTENANT GENERAL HATAZO ADACHI
(1884–1947)

Hatazo Adachi had a reputation for leading his men from the front, even when he reached the rank of general. The son of a poor samurai family, he joined the Japanese army and began service with the 1st Imperial Guards Division. He served in Manchuria in 1933, and then as a colonel in the Sino-Japanese war, where he was wounded by mortar fire. In 1941–42 he was Chief-of-Staff of the North China Area Army responsible for hunting down Chinese Communists. In November 1942, he was posted to Rabaul to take command of the 18th Army for the campaign on New Guinea. In 1944, his forces were isolated on the island, and were decimated by malaria and hunger. In September 1945, he surrendered and was charged with war crimes by the Australian government. Sentenced to life imprisonment, he committed ritual suicide with a paring knife on 10 September 1947.

RIGHT An American unit on the Soputa front, near the New Guinea port of Buna, carrying wounded comrades back to headquarters after 11 days' continuous combat during the campaign to drive Japanese forces out of the southern areas of the island.

20 NOVEMBER 1943—23 FEBRUARY 1944

ISLAND-HOPPING IN THE PACIFIC: GILBERT AND MARSHALL ISLANDS

The assault on New Guinea and Rabaul in the second half of 1943 was one wing of a two-pronged campaign. A second line of attack was launched through the Solomon Islands north of Guadalcanal and on into the central Pacific against the outlying Gilbert and Marshall islands, viewed as stepping-stones to the distant Marianas, which were within striking distance of Japan for the US Army Air Force's new generation of long-range heavy bombers, the B-29 Superfortress.

In June 1943, Admiral William Halsey's Third Fleet began the task of capturing the main islands of the southern Solomons. Rendova Island was taken on 30 June, then New Georgia was attacked and the base at Munda captured on 4–5 August. Japanese convoys sent to help the endangered garrisons were destroyed in two battles in the Kula Gulf

and the Vella Gulf, and on 1 November US forces, supported by the 3rd New Zealand Division, landed on the main island of Bougainville, where air bases could be set up to bomb the Japanese base at Rabaul. Japanese reinforcements were hastily sent to the island, where the Japanese garrison numbered around 37,500 men, but Halsey was able to call on extensive

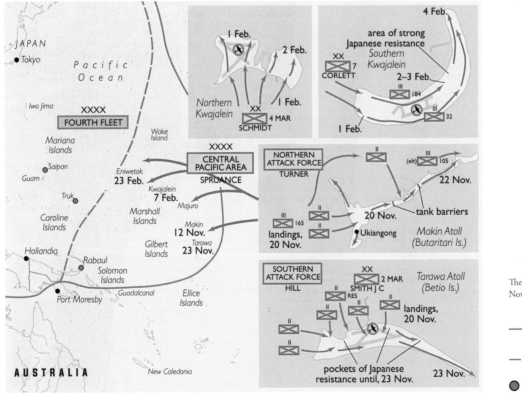

The Central Pacific,
November 1943–February 1944

Japanese occupied,
November 1943

Japanese occupied,
February 1944

Japanese base

THE BATTLE FOR TARAWA

The battle for the small island of Betio on the edge of Tarawa Atoll in the Gilbert Islands was one of the toughest battles of the Pacific War. Only 4,500 Japanese marines garrisoned the island, but they were well supplied and dug in to deep defensive positions, including 500 pillboxes and a network of concealed trenches. The US naval force that mounted the operation included no fewer than 17 aircraft carriers and 12 battleships and transported 35,000 US marines and soldiers. They attacked on 20 November 1943, but intense Japanese fire and difficult tidal waters pinned the invaders on the beaches. There followed three days of fierce fighting, but vastly superior manpower and supplies gradually allowed the American forces to gain the upper hand. At the end of the battle, only 17 Japanese soldiers were left alive, but a total of 1,009 US marines and sailors lost their lives and 2,101 were wounded, prompting strong criticism of the operation among the American public.

US Marines clear a Japanese pillbox on the Tarawa Atoll.

air support to contain the Japanese threat while an assault by two of his carriers on the powerful fleet of Vice Admiral Kurita at Rabaul forced a Japanese withdrawal. The Japanese were bottled up on Bougainville for the rest of the war, at the end of which *c.* 23,000 finally surrendered.

Further north, Admiral Nimitz prepared to assault the Gilbert and Marshall islands. A force of 200 ships was assembled, with 35,000 soldiers and marines and 6,000 vehicles. On 13 November, a sustained naval bombardment began against the Makin and Tarawa atolls in the Gilbert Islands. The attack, codenamed Operation "Galvanic", began on 20 November against Makin Atoll, which was secured by 23 November after limited but fierce fighting by a small Japanese garrison of 800 soldiers, which had no aircraft and was commanded by no one more senior than a first lieutenant. A Japanese submarine from Truk sank a US escort carrier, *Liscombe Bay*. Betio Island on Tarawa Atoll took the same time to secure, but only after bitter and costly fighting for both sides. Attention then shifted to the Marshall Islands further north, a German colony taken over as a mandate by the Japanese in 1919. The objective here was to capture the main Japanese base on Kwajalein Atoll in an operation codenamed "Flintlock". Rear Admiral Charles Pownall's Task Force 50 bombarded the Japanese positions more than a month before the assault took place, followed by heavy attacks from land-based aircraft.

On 1 February, an armada of 297 ships brought the US 7th Infantry Division to Kwajalein, while the 4th Marine Division went on to the Roi and Namur islands further to the north of the group. In total 85,000 troops were involved in the hope of avoiding the costly battles experienced in the Gilberts. After six days of heavy fighting, all three islands were secure; on Kwajalein only 265 Japanese soldiers were taken alive out of a garrison of 4,000. Nimitz then ordered a further operation against the Engei and Eniwotek atolls, 560 kilometres (350 miles) northwest of Kwajalein. Attacks here secured the islands between 18 and 23 February. The US naval forces were now within striking distance of the Marianas, and aircraft from the Marshalls could attack the main Japanese naval base at Truk. Although there was much argument over the merits of the island-hopping campaign, where tiny atolls were secured at a high cost in casualties, Nimitz was keen to push the central Pacific avenue to Japan as a more efficient, faster and ultimately less costly strategy than MacArthur's idea of attacking through the East Indies and the Philippines against heavy Japanese force concentrations. The result was a division of resources between two different campaigns, and a growing sense of rivalry between the army and navy over who would defeat Japan first.

22–25 NOVEMBER 1943
Cairo Conference of Churchill, Roosevelt and Chiang Kaishek discusses strategy for the Far East.

28 DECEMBER 1943
Italian city of Ortona is captured after bitter fighting along the Gustav Line.

4 JANUARY 1944
Red Army crosses the pre-1939 Polish border into German-occupied Europe.

27 JANUARY 1944
The Siege of Leningrad is finally lifted after the death of an estimated one million inhabitants.

15 FEBRUARY 1944
The monastery of Monte Cassino is heavily bombed by the Allies and completely destroyed.

17 FEBRUARY 1944
The capture of Kanyev Pocket leaves 55,000 Germans killed with 18,200 taken prisoner.

REAR ADMIRAL MARC A. MITSCHER
(1887–1947)

One of the pioneers of naval aviation in the US Navy, Marc Mitscher played an important part in driving the Japanese from the central Pacific during the Second World War. He joined the navy in 1906, transferring to the Aeronautics Section in 1915. He was one of three navy pilots who flew across the Atlantic in flying boats in 1919. He was assistant chief of the Bureau of Aeronautics from 1939 to 1941, and then took command of the aircraft carrier USS *Hornet* from which the Doolittle raid was launched against Japanese cities in April 1942. His carrier saw action at Midway, and in April 1943 he became Air Commander in the Solomons. He was appointed to command carrier Task Force 58 (later known as the Fast Carrier Task Force) which harried the Japanese in New Guinea and the Marianas and in March 1944 was promoted to Vice Admiral. At the end of the war he was appointed Deputy Chief of Naval Operations responsible for aviation, and in 1946 became Commander-in-Chief of the Atlantic Fleet.

ISLAND-HOPPING ACTION REPORT

The action report of 10 December 1943 from Admiral Raymond Spruance detailing the role of his Central Pacific Area fleet in the "island hopping" campaigns of November and December 1943. His carriers played a critical role in supplying air support for the brief islands campaigns.

SECRET DECLASSIFIED
DECLASSIFIED SECURITY INFORMATION

ORIGINAL

ACTION REPORT

COMMANDER CENTRAL PACIFIC FORCE

SERIAL 00156 10 DECEMBER 1943

REPORT ON GALVANIC OPERATIONS, ON 6 NOVEMBER - 8 DECEMBER 1943.

PRELIMINARY GENERAL REPORT, IN ADVANCE OF SUBORDINATE COMMANDERS' REPORTS, ON OCCUPATION OF MAKIN, TARAWA, APAMAMA AND STRIKES ON KWAJALEIN AND NAURU. COVERS FROM DEPARTURE OF FIRST COMBAT SHIPS THROUGH ATTACK ON NAURU.

61601

DIVISION OF NAVAL RECORDS AND HISTORY

Serial: 00156

SECRET
S E C R E T

10 DEC 1943

From:　　Commander Central Pacific Force, U.S. Pacific Fleet.
To　:　　Commander in Chief, U.S. Pacific Fleet.

Subject:　　GALVANIC Operations - report on.

1.　　The following is submitted as a general report on GALVANIC in advance of the detailed reports on that operation which will be made by Task Group and Task Force Commanders. Some of the statements made may, however, require modification in the light of information contained in these reports.

2.　　GALVANIC was carried out according to plan up to and including D day (20 November). After D day, the plans were less specific and more flexible, in order to allow for and to take advantage of the unknown element of enemy reaction. In general, the plans for the period following D day were carried out, except that such shifts were made in fueling and carrier areas as seemed likely to prevent interference by enemy aircraft and submarines. As vessels of the attack forces, both combatant and transport types, cleared the area to return to PEARL, the escorting DDs with them were reduced in numbers and the surplus returned to the captured bases to help overcome the existing shortage of screening vessels.

3.　　GALVANIC was favored by our obtaining a large element of tactical surprise, insofar as the approach of all task groups and task forces to their various objectives was concerned. So far as is known, the DALE and the three LSTs which she was escorting to MAKIN were the only elements of the two attack forces (TF 52 and 53) picked up by the enemy in advance of their arrival at MAKIN and TARAWA. The DALE group was picked up by air search on D - 1 day, but fortunately received no damage.

4.　　It appears probable that the South Pacific operations against EMPRESS AUGUSTA BAY on BOUGAINVILLE and the rehearsals at EFATE of Task Force 53 may have kept the Japanese high command uncertain up until D day as to where our blow was to be struck. Whatever the cause, the delay on the part of the enemy in sending submarines into the GILBERTS and in reinforcing his striking air strength in the MARSHALLS enabled us to capture our objectives with much less interference from these arms than might have been anticipated.

5.　　The damage inflicted on enemy cruisers and destroyers in RABAUL by the SARATOGA and PRINCETON air attacks on 5 November had the expected result of immobilizing the main elements of the Japanese fleet because of lack of light forces, and of preventing any interference with GALVANIC by enemy surface forces.

-1-

SECRET
S E C R E T

CENTRAL PACIFIC FORCE
UNITED STATES PACIFIC FLEET
FLAGSHIP OF THE COMMANDER

Subject:　　GALVANIC Operations - report on.

6.　　Enemy submarine action was slow in developing. Our only casualty from submarines was the unfortunate sinking, early on the morning of 24 November, of the LISCOME BAY off MAKIN, with the regrettable loss of Rear Admiral Mullinix, Captain Wiltsie, and a large proportion of her officers and men. Reports indicate that the torpedo hit produced an internal explosion which caused the ship practically to disintegrate.

7.　　Off TARAWA, enemy submarines approached the transport area, but screening and vigorous counter measures prevented any attacks on our ships there. Moderate to fresh surface winds provided excellent sound conditions. One Japanese submarine was definitely sunk by the MEADE and the FRAZIER in this area with three men taken prisoner from her. Several other submarines were detected and attacked by aircraft and destroyers with undetermined, but apparently good, results.

8.　　Enemy air attacks were kept down by strikes made by our shore based air from CANTON and the ELLICE Islands on NAURU, JALUIT, MILLE, TAROA and WOTJE and by our carrier air on NAURU, JALUIT and MILLE. As a result of these strikes, no enemy air interference came from NAURU, and a minimum was staged through MILLE from other bases further north in the MARSHALLS. Enemy seaplanes based on JALUIT did little of value for the enemy.

9.　　The only casualty suffered by our ships from air attack in the GILBERTS was the torpedoing of the INDEPENDENCE early on the evening of 20 November in the area to the southwest of TARAWA. Fortunately, the INDEPENDENCE was able to proceed, with one engine-room in commission, to FUNAFUTI for emergency repairs at that base prior to going on to PEARL.

10.　　Other attacks, some of them very vigorous, were made on our carrier task groups by enemy medium bombers armed with both torpedoes and bombs, but, through skillful maneuvering, gunfire and, in the case of Admiral Radford's Task Group, the use of carrier night fighters, no damage was inflicted on any of our ships.

11.　　It is significant that the enemy attempted no daylight air attacks. Nuisance night raids on TARAWA were started with the advent of a suitable moon in December, but by this time the airfield was in use and searchlights, AA batteries and radars set up and functioning.

12.　　Subsequent attacks on enemy air bases were made by two carrier task groups under Rear Admirals Pownall and Montgomery which bombed KWAJALEIN and WOTJE on 4 December; and by a battleship and carrier task group under Rear Admiral Lee which bombed and bombarded NAURU on 8 December. Both of these attacks were made after the ships involved had completed the tasks assigned them in GALVANIC and while returning to their bases at PEARL and the NEW HEBRIDES,

-2-

SECRET
S E C R E T

CENTRAL PACIFIC FORCE
UNITED STATES PACIFIC FLEET
FLAGSHIP OF THE COMMANDER

Subject:　　GALVANIC Operations - report on.

respectively. Carrier air groups in these task forces had their flight crew and aircraft losses made up by planes from the SARATOGA, PRINCETON, INDEPENDENCE and CarDiv 22 before proceeding on these attacks. At the same time, a reassignment of cruisers and battleships was made to these task groups on the basis of their ultimate destinations on the conclusion of GALVANIC.

13.　　As directed by the Commander in Chief, U.S. Pacific Fleet, the main attack in the MARSHALLS on 4 December under Rear Admiral Pownall was directed against KWAJALEIN, where enemy naval and merchant type ships, aircraft and shore installations were heavily struck with torpedoes and bombs. A lighter attack was made on WOTJE. TAROA was not attacked. In withdrawing, our two carrier task groups were attacked by enemy aircraft in strength. As a result, the LEXINGTON was hit with one torpedo, but was able to proceed to PEARL under her own power.

14.　　No details have been received as yet of the bombing and bombardment of NAURU conducted by Rear Admiral Lee on 8 December.

15.　　The weather in the GILBERTS during the attack phase of GALVANIC was most favorable for us. The sea was smooth, but an eastsoutheasterly wind of 12 - 15 knots prevailed. This wind greatly facilitated our carrier air operations; reduced by one half the fuel expenditure of the carrier task groups during those days when air operations were at a maximum from what it would have been with the light airs that came a few days later; and so permitted us to build up a fuel reserve that removed any concern over shortage of fuel.

16.　　The equatorial front during most of GALVANIC lay south of JALUIT and MILLE and interfered with enemy air operations from those bases. Only occasionally did it move as far south as MAKIN.

17.　　Of the lessons learned as a result of GALVANIC, the chief and most expensive ones came from the assault and capture of BETIO Island, TARAWA. These are of a technical nature and involve matters such as: types of landing craft best suited for a movement over fringing coral reefs; the amount of preliminary bombing and bombardment required in preparation for the landing; kinds of bombs and shells to be used; and tactics and equipment of the landing force. Matters such as these must be studied and discussed thoroughly by the best qualified personnel before sound conclusions can be reached.

18.　　The capture of both MAKIN and TARAWA has emphasized the necessity for a full and detailed reconnaissance of heavily defended enemy bases before their capture is attempted. This reconnaissance must include the lagoons and their beaches, if a lagoon landing is to be made. The presence or absence of a fringing coral reef inside the lagoon where the landing is to be made is a matter of the utmost importance in its effect on the types of landing craft to be used. Tidal conditions must also be known. All of this information can best

- 3 -

SECRET
S E C R E T

CENTRAL PACIFIC FORCE
UNITED STATES PACIFIC FLEET
FLAGSHIP OF THE COMMANDER

Subject:　　GALVANIC Operations - report on.

be obtained by repeated observation and photography from aircraft and submarines.

19.　　The GALVANIC operation proper started on 6 November with the departure for the objectives of the first of the combatant units involved. D day was 20 November. The landing of the APAMAMA garrison was completed on 7 December. The last blow by naval units was struck at NAURU on 8 December (all west longitude dates).

20.　　While GALVANIC itself thus occupied one month, the preliminary planning, movement of ships, and training of units took up a period slightly greater than the preceding two months. It is estimated that the consolidation and building up of our newly occupied bases in the GILBERTS will require a succeeding period of from one to two months before these bases can be effectively used to support a successive operation.

21.　　Throughout GALVANIC the Commander Central Pacific Force was particularly gratified by the intelligent initiative displayed by all task force, group and unit commanders. All hands contributed their best efforts to the carrying out of our mission.

22.　　The high light of the campaign, and the part that will be longest remembered in American history, was the magnificent courage and tenacity of the Second Marine Division in carrying on their assault on BETIO Island for a period of four days after suffering staggering losses. Nothing in the record of the Marine Corps can exceed the heroism displayed at TARAWA by the officers and men of the Second Marine Division and by the naval units that accompanied them in their landing.

R. A. SPRUANCE.

Encl: Two copies.

27

17 JANUARY–18 MAY 1944

THE BATTLE FOR MONTE CASSINO

The key to breaking the German grip on south-central Italy was the heavily defended area around Cassino and the valleys of the Liri and Rapido rivers. This was the setting for one of the most bitterly contested struggles of the war in the west which led to the complete destruction of the ancient Benedictine monastery of Monte Cassino, set high on an outcrop of mountainside above the town of Cassino.

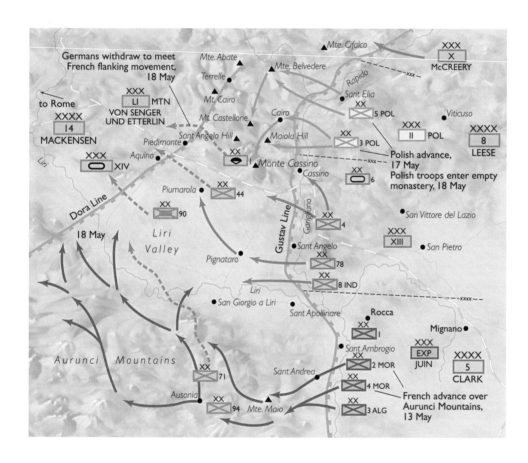

Monte Cassino, 13–18 May 1944

The battle for Cassino lasted five months and involved four major operations. The German 14th Panzer Corps, under General von Senger und Etterlin, bore the brunt of the defence, dug in to the rugged landscape and valley sides that made up this part of the Gustav Line. The Allied plan, set out in a directive from Alexander's headquarters on 8 November 1943, was to destroy German forces in the Liri valley and to approach Rome from the south, in conjunction with a landing at Anzio designed to roll up the German front. Early attacks in December on the German defences showed how difficult the assault would be with Allied forces that were battle-worn after the hard drive up from Sicily.

A photograph of the Benedictine monastery of Monte Cassino taken c.1927. The site had been a monastery since the 6th century AD and was a building of exceptional architectural and religious significance. German forces promised not to occupy the building and did not do so until it had been destroyed by Allied bombing.

The opening battle began on 17 January 1944 when British forces tried to cross the River Garigliano and the Americans the River Rapido three days later. Small bridgeheads were secured against fierce resistance and the US 5th Army began a slow ascent towards the monastery before heavy losses forced a halt on mountains to the northeast while the French Expeditionary Corps made progress to the north. But on 11 February the first attack was called off, with total Allied casualties of 14,000, sustained

11 JANUARY 1944
Former Italian Fascist foreign minister Count Ciano is shot for treason by Mussolini's new regime in northern Italy.

14 JANUARY 1944
Allied bombers attack Bulgarian capital Sofia from Mediterranean bases.

18 FEBRUARY 1944
US marines land on Eniwetok and Engei atolls in the Marshall Islands, securing both within six days.

6 MARCH 1944
Major American bombing raid on Berlin with 700 planes from 8th Air Force, resulting in losses of 69 aircraft.

2 APRIL 1944
Soviet forces begin the invasion of Romania, Germany's Axis ally.

17 APRIL 1944
Japanese army in China launches Operation "Ichi-Go" in Henan province, the start of seven months of fighting.

GENERAL FRIDOLIN VON SENGER UND ETTERLIN
(1891–1963)

The son of a German aristocratic family, von Senger und Etterlin joined the army in 1910 before going to Oxford University as a Rhodes Scholar. He served through the First World War and stayed on in the postwar army as commander of a cavalry regiment. He reached the rank of colonel by 1939 and fought in the Battle of France in command of his own mobile brigade. In October 1942, he commanded the 17th Panzer Division in southern Russia. As a lieutenant general he commanded German forces in Sicily in July and August 1943. On mainland Italy he commanded the 14th Panzer Corps and became a general of Panzer troops on 1 January 1944. He was opposed to Hitler but took no part in the assassination plot of July 1944. After the war he became a leading expert on German armoured forces and vehicles.

in weeks of harsh weather and fierce fighting. A second assault was planned a week later using General Freyberg's New Zealand Corps, but Freyberg, anxious that German troops would use the monastery as a fortress, requested a preliminary bombing attack. Clark was unwilling, but he was overruled by Alexander, the Allied commander in Italy. On 15 February, 229 bombers pulverized the monastery into ruins.

It was only then that the German forces moved into the rubble, which provided good defensive positions. The only inhabitants of the monastery had been Italian civilians and a number of monks sheltering from the conflict, and between 300 and 400 were killed. On the night of 17 February, the New Zealanders attacked the Cassino railway station while the 4th Indian Division attacked the monastery hill. After three days the offensive was called off after achieving almost nothing. Alexander then planned to wait until the spring to launch a more carefully prepared assault, but under pressure from London and Washington to give relief to the threatened Anzio beachhead, a third assault on Cassino was tried. After a massive air bombardment which turned Cassino into a ruin, the New Zealand Corps again tried to storm the town between 15 and 23 March, but after taking 4,000 casualties and battered by appalling weather, the attack was called off.

The final assault was postponed until May. Alexander prepared a major operation, codenamed "Diadem", designed finally to unhinge the German line. The French forces in the south pushed across the Garigliano River and the Aurunci Mountains, threatening the whole south of the German line. The British 8th Army assaulted and finally captured Cassino, while on 17 May the Polish 2nd Corps under General Anders assaulted the monastery and, after heavy hand-to-hand fighting and losses of 3,500 men, occupied it on 18 May as German forces withdrew. The fourth Cassino battle persuaded Kesselring that his position was untenable and he began moving his forces back to the Gothic Line, north of Florence. Clark's 5th Army met up with Truscott's Anzio forces on 25 May. In the end, victory at Cassino was needed to rescue the Anzio operation, the opposite of what had been intended when the operations to break the Gustav Line were first launched late in 1943.

RIGHT Troops of the Polish 2nd Corps climbing the slopes of the monastery hill in May 1944. The Polish units took terrible casualties in the assault but fought with exceptional courage.

GENERAL WLADYSLAW ANDERS
(1892–1970)

General Anders became famous in the Second World War as the leader of the Polish 2nd Corps which captured the monastery of Monte Cassino. The son of a German father, he was born in Russian-ruled Poland and fought in the tsar's army against the Germans during the First World War. After the war, he joined the army of the new Polish state as a cavalry commander. He was captured by the Red Army in September 1939 when Poland was invaded from the east, and imprisoned and tortured (though, unlike thousands of other Polish officers, not murdered). He was freed in July 1941 and then led a large force of Poles through Iran and Iraq, where they met up with British forces and formed a Polish army corps. He fought in Italy and after the war stayed in Britain as a member of the Polish government-in-exile. He was buried in the cemetery at Monte Cassino among the soldiers he had led there.

OPPOSITE A New Zealand anti-tank gun in action on 15 March 1944 during the attempt by the New Zealand Corps to seize the hill and monastery. After heavy casualties they were forced to withdraw.

LEFT Polish and British flags fly side by side above the monastery of Monte Cassino on 18 May 1944 after the German withdrawal. The capture of Monte Cassino paved the way for a rapid advance past Rome to Florence.

6 JUNE 1944

D-DAY

The invasion of Normandy on 6 June 1944 was the culmination of years of strategic argument and operational preparation by the two western Allies, Britain and the United States. In 1942, the US Army chief, General Marshall, wanted commitment to a cross-Channel Operation "Roundup" in the spring of 1943 following the build-up of American forces in Britain. British leaders were never enthusiastic about this plan and the decision to invade first North Africa (November 1942) and then Sicily (July 1943) made any major operation in northern Europe impossible. In the spring of 1943, a planning staff was finally established under the British Lieutenant General Frederick Morgan to prepare for a possible invasion in May 1944. Over the course of 1943 this option hardened into a definite plan to invade on a narrow front in Normandy, but only at the Quebec Conference in August 1943 was the decision to launch what was called Operation "Overlord" finally confirmed. Over the winter of 1943–44 British leaders still harboured doubts and preferred a more peripheral strategy in the Mediterranean to a head-on collision with German forces in France.

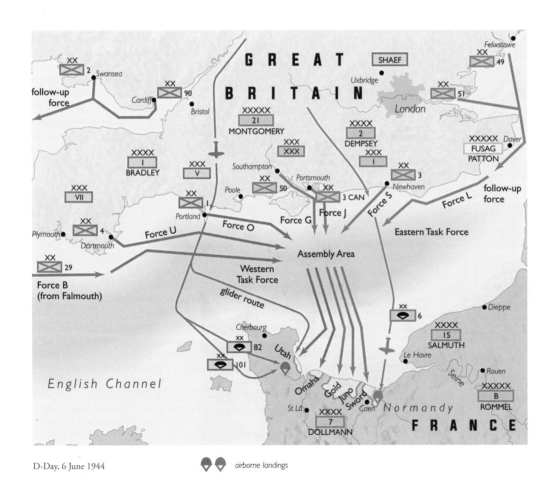

D-Day, 6 June 1944   airborne landings

The planning and preparation speeded up after Quebec. General Eisenhower was appointed the supreme commander for "Overlord" and General Bernard Montgomery was chosen as the army commander-in-chief in the field. Both men realized that the original plan to attack on a narrow front with a handful of divisions would not work. The eventual plan foresaw an attack on a broader front with six divisions on five separate beaches, to be followed up with a force of 37 divisions which would break out and defeat the German armies in France. On 1 February, the staff planners agreed on the basis of the tides that 31 May would be D-Day, with an option for 5, 6 or 7 June if the weather proved difficult in May. The problem of supplying the beachhead was solved by the development of artificial harbours or "mulberries" that were to be towed in parts across the Channel and assembled close to the front line. The supply and transportation for D-Day was organized under the naval Operation "Neptune" commanded by the Royal Navy's Admiral Ramsay, who led 7,000 warships, transports and small boats towards the coast of France on the eventual day of the invasion.

1 JUNE 1944
French resistance alerted to D-Day and begin guerrilla operations.

4 JUNE 1944
Allied forces enter Rome.

4 JUNE 1944
Poor weather forces postponement of D-Day from 5 June.

10 JUNE 1944
Red Army begins major operation against Finnish forces.

10 JUNE 1944
Waffen-SS forces destroy French village of Oradour and murder 642 men, women and children.

15 JUNE 1944
US forces land on the island of Saipan.

BELOW A German heavy gun battery overlooking the English Channel, built in April 1942. It bears the name "Batterie Todt" in honour of Fritz Todt, leader of the Todt Organization which built the Atlantic Wall defences. He was also Minister of Munitions before his death in an air crash in February 1942.

Sword Beach on the morning of 6 June 1944. Support troops of the 3rd British Infantry Division gather near La Breche under light artillery attack to prepare to move off the beach inland to secure a perimeter around the beachhead.

FIELD MARSHAL GERD VON RUNDSTEDT
(1875–1953)

One of the most outstanding German army leaders of the war, von Rundstedt was the overall commander of German forces in the West at the time of the Normandy invasion. He came from a distinguished Prussian military family and was a successful and much-decorated soldier by the time Hitler came to power. He was made a full general in 1938 and commanded Army Group South for the invasion of Poland and Army Group A for the invasion of France. He was created Field Marshal in July 1940 and became Commander-in-Chief West until recalled to lead Army Group South in the Barbarossa campaign. He was sacked for retreating from Rostov in December 1941, but reinstated as C-in-C West from March 1942 to July 1944 and again from September 1944 to March 1945. Though a private critic of Hitler's strategy, he was publicly loyal throughout the war. He was arrested at the end of the war and was to be tried for war crimes but ill health led to his early release in 1949.

To oppose the Allied invasion the German army had constructed a complex web of defences across northern France known as the Atlantic Wall. Command of the German armies in the field was given to Field Marshal Rommel but his view that the best way to repel invasion was on the beaches clashed with his immediate superior, Field Marshal von Rundstedt, who wanted the mobile forces instead held back from the coast to avoid Allied air and naval power but ready to launch an annihilating counter-offensive. Hitler intervened and divided the mobile forces so that neither strategy could work well, with too few mobile divisions on the coast yet too few in reserve. By June 1944, there were 58 divisions spread out over the whole of France. Rommel expected invasion in the Pas-de-Calais in northeastern France and a diversionary attack in Normandy. Hence, by June 1944 there were 14 divisions in General Dollmann's 7th Army in Normandy, but 20 divisions along the coast around Calais. Thanks to a successful deception plan, planted in German minds by double-agents working in Britain, most German military planners, and Hitler too, expected the main weight of attack across the shortest stretch of Channel towards Calais. When Allied forces finally sailed for Normandy, the German defence was caught almost entirely by surprise.

After months of preparation the date for invasion was fixed in mid-May for 5 June. The United States 1st Army under Lieutenant General Omar Bradley was to attack two beaches codenamed "Omaha" and "Utah", while

A panorama of "Omaha" Beach on D-Day after it had been secured by units of the US First Army. Tank-carrying landing craft can be seen drawn up on the beach unloading their vehicles directly onto the shore. By evening over 130,000 men had been landed on the beaches with generous supplies of equipment.

the British 2nd Army under Lieutenant General Miles Dempsey attacked "Juno", "Gold" and "Sword" beaches. Poor weather forced postponement until 6 June, but early that morning the huge armada of warships and smaller craft approached the French coast; there then began a ferocious bombardment, first with 2,856 heavy bombers, then with naval gunfire and finally with waves of fighter-bombers. So heavy was the bombardment that in the British sector the fight for the beaches was easily won and by the end of the day a bridgehead several kilometres deep had been captured and defended against limited German counter-attacks. American forces had the same success at "Utah", landing against only light fire and carving out a 10-kilometre (6-mile) bridgehead by the end of the day with only 197 casualties. On "Omaha" beach there was a harder battle, since the initial bombardment had failed to hit the defences effectively and high cliffs made rapid movement difficult. By the end of the day the beach was held, but little more, and with around 2,000 casualties. During the day a total of 130,000 men were landed successfully in Normandy for the overall price of around 10,300 casualties from all causes.

ADMIRAL BERTRAM RAMSAY
(1883–1945)

Admiral Ramsay was the naval mastermind behind first the Dunkirk evacuations and then the naval component of the D-Day operations. He joined the Royal Navy in 1898 and served as a lieutenant commander in the Dover Patrol between 1915 and 1918. He retired as a rear admiral in 1938 after disagreements with his immediate superior but was recalled to active duty as flag officer, Dover, between August 1939 and 1942. He was deputy naval commander for the Torch landings in November 1942, and commander of the Eastern Task Force for the invasion of Sicily before his appointment as Allied naval commander-in-chief for the invasion of France. He was a popular, efficient and tough-minded commander, who achieved remarkable success in organizing the naval back-up for the invasion. He died in an air crash on 2 January 1945.

MONTGOMERY'S D-DAY PLANS

Field Marshal Montgomery's handwritten notes for D-Day, 6 June 1944. The notes show his direct and uncomplicated approach to what promised to be a complex and difficult operation. The forces under his command did achieve what was required – a quick disembarkation and consolidation of the beachhead.

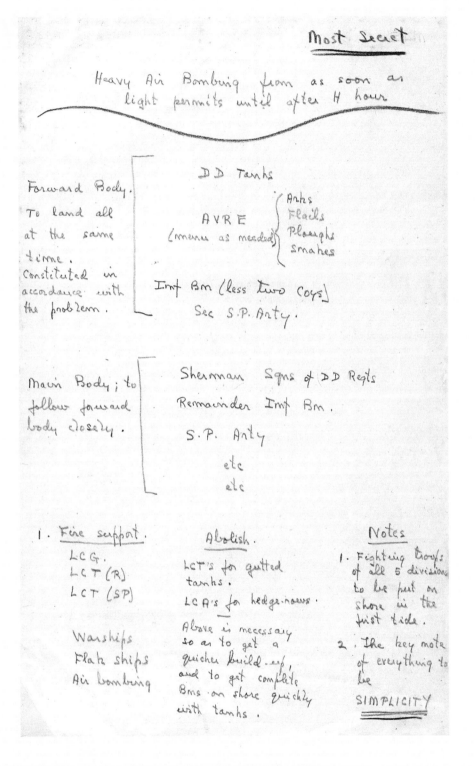

Most Secret

Heavy Air Bombing from as soon as light permits until after H hour

Forward Body.
To land all at the same time.
Constituted in accordance with the problem.

DD Tanks

AVRE
(menu as needed)
{ Arks
Flails
Ploughs
Snakes }

Inf Bn (less two Coys)
Sec S.P. Arty.

Main Body; to follow forward body closely.

Sherman Sqns of DD Regts
Remainder Inf Bn.
S.P. Arty
etc
etc

1. Fire support.
LCG.
LCT (R)
LCT (SP)

Warships
Flak ships
Air bombing

Abolish.
LCT's for gutted tanks.
LCA's for hedge-rows.

Above is necessary so as to get a quicker build-up, and to get complete Bns on shore quickly with tanks.

Notes
1. Fighting troops of all 5 divisions to be put on shore in the first tide.

2. The key note of everything to be SIMPLICITY

39

7 JUNE–25 JULY 1944

BATTLE FOR NORMANDY

The lodgement in Normandy was secure enough by 7 June to prevent a strategic catastrophe, but the progress of the campaign over the following weeks was very much slower than the original plans for "Overlord" had envisaged. By 11 June, there were 326,000 men ashore supported by 54,000 vehicles; by the middle of the month more than 500,000 men, organized in 19 divisions, had been landed. But even with complete command of the air, Montgomery's forces failed to take the city of Caen, while in the western invasion area Bradley's First US Army finally seized the Cotentin Peninsula and captured the port of Cherbourg after more than three weeks of fighting against comparatively light German resistance.

Montgomery's plan was to force the Germans to concentrate most of their force, including the valuable Panzer divisions, on the front around Caen, so allowing Bradley to break out in the west and swing in a long encirclement behind German armies engaged against the British and Canadians. The operational skills of Rommel's forces combined with the difficult terrain (swampy in places or covered with thick, high hedgerows known as *bocage*) made it difficult for the Allies to bring their advantages to bear. When a fierce gale destroyed one of the floating "Mulberry"

harbours on 19–20 June, the supply of equipment and men temporarily dried up and Rommel took the opportunity to concentrate his armour for a counter-offensive around Caen, which he launched on 1 July. The attack was repulsed in the heaviest fighting since D-Day, but the failure to secure Caen and speed up the collapse of German resistance led to strained relations between Montgomery and a frustrated Eisenhower, who had expected a quick break-out once the lodgement was sufficiently secure and reinforced.

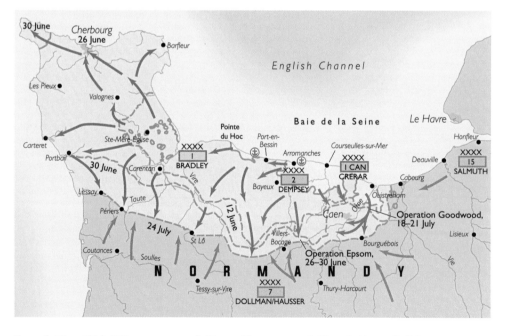

Normandy, 7 June–24 July 1944   —— *front line, a.m. 7 June*   - - - *front lines, with date*   ⚓ *Mulberry*

19–20 JUNE 1944
Battle of the Philippine Sea results in heavy losses for the Japanese fleet and naval air power.

3 JULY 1944
Battle of Imphal on the Indian-Burmese border ends in a rout for the Japanese army.

18 JULY 1944
The Japanese prime minister, General Tojo, resigns following Japanese defeat at Saipan.

24 JULY
Soviet forces liberate the German extermination camp at Majdanek in their rapid advance across Belorussia and eastern Poland.

Vehicles drive ashore over the long pontoon bridges of the "Mulberry" harbour at Arromanches in August 1944. Before a major port was secured much Allied equipment was shipped through the artificial harbours. The other harbour, at St Laurent, was damaged in a gale in June and could no longer be used, placing even greater strain on Arromanches.

On 7 July, Montgomery began a major operation of his own to seize Caen and break the German line. Following a massive aerial bombardment, which made progress through the rubble-strewn streets difficult, the town was captured, but Rommel withdrew to a series of five defensive lines constructed to the south, including a concentrated gun line of the formidable "tank-busting" 88-millimetre anti-aircraft guns

along the Bourguebus Ridge. Urged on by Eisenhower, Montgomery then planned a second operation codenamed "Goodwood" to attack the German defensive zone. The operation was scheduled for 18 July; the day before, Rommel was severely injured when his car was strafed by British aircraft, and his command was assumed by Field Marshal von Kluge. On 18 July, the attack began with the heaviest air bombardment

ABOVE Royal Engineers' blue ensign flown from a "Mulberry" harbour pierhead off Arromanches, Normandy.

GENERAL OMAR BRADLEY
(1893–1981)

Omar Bradley became one of the most distinguished American army commanders during the Second World War. He did not see combat in the First World War but in the interwar years his qualities as an infantry commander brought him promotion to brigadier general by 1941. He was appointed deputy commander of Patton's 2nd US Corps in North Africa in 1943 and in April took over full command, playing an important role in completing the destruction of Axis forces there. He commanded the Corps in Sicily but then in September 1943 arrived in Britain where, thanks to his growing reputation as a cool-headed commander with considerable tactical flair, he eventually took over First US Army for the Normandy landings. During the campaign in France it was Patton (commander 3rd Army) who now played deputy to Bradley (commander of 12th US Army Group). Bradley commanded US land forces from Normandy to the final defeat of Germany and was promoted to four-star general in March 1945 and, eventually, to general of the army in 1950.

of the campaign followed by fierce fighting all through the villages on the Bourguebus Ridge. Torrential rain two days later brought the operation to a halt with the German gun line still intact, but the German command had been forced to move two of the armoured divisions facing Bradley in the west to reinforce the eastern contest. This made it possible for the Americans to break out of Normandy a few days later.

Despite their defensive success, German commanders knew that they could not survive the rate of attrition of German forces. Between D-Day and "Goodwood" they had lost 2,117 tanks and 113,000 men, and had been sent only 17 tanks and 10,000 men as replacements. Von Kluge wanted to move the front back in an orderly retreat across France, but Hitler insisted that the 7th Army should stand and fight where it was. Allied forces possessed around 4,500 tanks by late July against only 850 German, all but 190 of them facing Montgomery south of Caen. Allied air superiority was overwhelming – around 12,000 aircraft against a total of 1,000 German planes sent to France during June and July, which were shot out of the skies or destroyed at their bases. The defensive circle around the Allies in Normandy was a brittle one by the end of July. Montgomery's strategy had worked sufficiently to create conditions where a final push would produce a German collapse, but it operated too slowly for a supreme commander who wanted quick results. It was Eisenhower's sense of urgency against Montgomery's battlefield prudence that created the postwar myth that the British command failed in Normandy. In reality, the two months of attritional warfare had already broken the back of the German war effort in the West. Within a month almost the whole of France would be in Allied hands.

On 7 July 1944, 467 heavy bombers of the RAF made a devastating attack on the French town of Caen before beginning the operation to capture it from the German 7th Army. Here, a British soldier on 10 July carries a small girl through the ruins of the city. The rubble made it harder for Allied forces to move through the streets, which were abandoned by the Germans on 9 July.

GENERAL HENRY CRERAR
(1888–1965)

As chief of the Canadian General Staff, Henry Crerar played an important role from 1941 in raising and organizing a large Canadian army for the campaigns in Europe. A career artillery officer who fought through the First World War, Crerar was appointed to command the 2nd Canadian Division and then the 1st Canadian Corps in the Italian campaign. At the end of 1943, he was appointed Commander-in-Chief of the 1st Canadian Army and led the Canadian component in the invasion of Normandy. Except for a brief period of medical leave, he commanded the Canadian armies for the liberation of France and the invasion of northern Germany. His reputation rested on his administrative and political skills rather than on his battlefield performance, which Montgomery rated poorly. After the war he held a number of diplomatic posts in Czechoslovakia, Japan and the Netherlands.

D-DAY TO "MARKET GARDEN"

Part of the diary of Sergeant G.E. Hughes of the 1st Battalion, Royal Hampshire Regiment, British 50th Division, covering the period from D-Day to Operation "Market Garden" in September 1944. He describes the battles around Caen in mid-July as "Days of Hell".

JUNE 1944

4 Sun—Trinity Sunday
Mass 1000 hrs Must be near D DAY now roll on let's get it over with.

5 Mon
D DAY TOMORROW EVERY BODY QUITE EXCITED. WE LAND AT Arromanches Clear 3 Villages & Bayeux

6 Tues—Trinity Law Sittings begin. Full Moon
06:00 got in LCA, SEA VERY ROUGH HIT THE Beaches at 0720 HRS murderous fire, losses high I was lucky T God, cleared 3 Villages, terrible fighting and partly night.

7 Wed Still going dug in at 0200 away again at 05.30 no Food, writing few notes before we go into another village. CO and adjutant killed P Sgt lost I do P Sgt more later →

JUNE 1944

Passed through Bayeux last night took up Position last night Dive Bombers about 2 too snipers MONTY & DIV COMMANDER CONGRATULATES BATT

11 Sun—1st after Trinity. S. Barnabas
contact with enemy lost three of my Platoon very lucky T God only had 5 hrs sleep in 3 days.

12 Mon Ship day unbearable Mortar fire & wood fighting many casualties T God I survived another day.

13 Tues—Last Quarter
Just had my first meal since Monday morning up all night everyone in a terrible state I keep on thinking of Whiddy

14 Wed Counter attacked by Jerry from woods, Mortar fire, 13 of my Platoon killed or missing after heavy fighting, yesterday CSM also wounded also Lce O.C killed

JUNE 1944

18 Sun—2nd after Trinity. Waterloo, 1815
Day of Hell Counter attack

19 Mon
Day of Hell Counter Attack

20 Tues—New Moon
Day of Hell Advanced; counter Attacked

21 Wed—Longest Day
Quiet Day we have been fighting near Tilley Bay one charge letter I shelled all day from Home

JUNE 1944

8 Thur 7.30 fire coming from village, Village cleared Prisoners taken Night quite good but Germans snipers lurking in wood

9 Fri had 2 hrs sleep since the 6th seems hot. 06.00 hrs Went on wood clearing. Germans had flown, only one killed for our mornings work we are now about 8 to 10 miles in land of Armoured Div

10 Sat—s.r. 3.43, s.s. 8.15 ahead Joan Darling I have got back you bet of my thoughts I have come so far, we have lost some good men our brigade was only one to gain full objective on D DAY.

Mems the french people gave us a good welcome, had wine Our casualties high the landing was terrible had a near miss

JUNE 1944

I am one mass of scratches Advanced under creeping Barrage for 3 miles drove Jerry Back. it is hell here, 3 Tiger Tanks come up to lines during night I out action, the sobbing sisters keep on coming over, 2 Back

15 Thur

16 Fri Received letter from home, wrote to Joan & Mum We are resting in woods front line 3 miles away Brigade in our left going in 7th Armoured Div doing well

17 Sat—s.r. 3.42, s.s. 8.19
Still Resting prelude to another attack took patrol out over battle area to locate dead had some Wine & Cherries

Mems Monday nights news said Roosevelt troops were having it very sticky next, little did they know we have been fighting for our lives since landing

JUNE 1944

22 Thur Out on patrol got within 35 yds of Tiger before spotting it got back safe T God Shelled to blazes feeling tired out

23 Fri No Sleep last night exchange of fire out on patrol all day went on O P for 4 hrs stand too all night casualties

24 Sat—S. John Baptist. Midsummer Day (Quarter Day) s.r. 3.43, s.s. 8.21
O P to now all right 14.00 hrs Just had a good dinner Chickhen. May to go back to CCS Malaria,

Mems We all expect to have a leave soon how true I don't know Just about had enough after 19 days.

3 Sun—13th after Trinity
Great Britain declared war on Germany, 1939

Visited Amiens
Yesterday.
The Cathedral is a lovely
place

4 Mon We have little chance
of catching up with the
Batt. for a few days
now, I passed through
Arras today

5 Tues Slept at School teacher
home for two nights
very nice people
on patrol good time
people here much better
than Normandy Living

6 Wed Said goodbye to
good friends in Lieu?
they gave us everything
possible to make us
at home, were sorry to leave

10 Sun—14th after Trinity

I have just wrote to my Darling
also Mum, waiting to move
on again.

11 Mon Crossed Albert Canal
near Dutch border.
Felt shell over also
a few planes dropped
bombs.

12 Tues Good day.
Shells over but afternoon
all quiet, had plenty of mail
Baby takes like me. Ha ha

13 Wed
Moving towards
the Dutch border

17 Sun—15th after Trinity. Ember Week
● New Moon
WE STARTED BIG ATTACK FROM THE ESCAUT CANAL

Big Attack today to
enlarge Bridgehead
what a hiding Jerry
has coming.

18 Mon—Ramadân ends. Jewish Year 5705 begins
Mothers Birthday
We put in attack from Bridghead
it was hell let loose, this drive
will take us right through Holland
we are now 2 mile from border.

19 Tues We only lost 1 killed and 5
wounded but the Jerries lay in
masses all over the place
we had a attack by Jerry plains
they tried for the bridge but
missed, pushed dead before going into
but Victoria.

20 Wed—Ember Day
a quiet day the columns have
been going up since the break
through, had a look at some of
the Jerris also buried some

7 Thur Travelling all day
Crossed French border to Belgium
the welcome in Brussels
was great the streets were
packed, cigars grapes, flowers
were showered at us

8 Fri Waiting for transport
to cut out the Batt.
arrived at Antwerp
at night, good time
Champagne + supper

9 Sat—(Last Quarter
s.r. 5.23, s.s. 6.29
Got on transport
arrived at new place
waiting for next move
got good news often
Baby Son born 26th Sept

Mems What a Welcome
we had in Brussels
the people went mad
giving us wine cigars
toffees etc., a fine place

14 Thur
Mortared & Shelled
Letters from Joan,
Baby is lovely

15 Fri
Crossed second
canal formed a
bridgehead time
bomb taken away
just in time

16 Sat—s.r. 5.36, s.s. 6.25
Jerry attack of 20
18 killed or captured
Mortar + Shelled
all day. Letters from J.

Mems

21 Thur—S. Matthew
We jumped to mens life again today
had two letters from J and one just
one from Mum, of Joan taken
over another Platoon all new
chaps from England.

22 Fri—Ember Day
Fighting along road
Jerry bitter point up
with panzerfaust
crossed canal

23 Sat—Ember Day. Autumnal Equinox
s.r. 5.47, s.s. 5.57
Plenty of fighting
men all out but
have cleared it again

Mems Had bacon eggs and
cheese at Joan's good people
they are very kind. I helped
to bury them men who had
had a lot to do along today
with us soldiers.

13 JUNE 1944—29 MARCH 1945
THE V-WEAPONS CAMPAIGN

Under the impact of heavier Allied bombing attacks in 1942 and 1943, Adolf Hitler searched for some new weapon that could be used to attack British cities and perhaps force the Allies to end their bombing campaign. Two projects appealed particularly to Hitler as weapons of revenge (or *Vergeltungswaffen*): the first was a pilotless flying bomb, the Fieseler-Fi103, developed by the German air force; the second was the first successful ballistic missile, the A-4 rocket, developed by a team of scientists at the research station set up at Peenemünde on the north German coast. The two weapons were known as the V-1 and V-2, the "V" standing for vengeance (*Vergeltung*) in German.

The rocket first flew successfully in October 1942 but there were many technical problems to be overcome with the liquid-fuelled engine and the guidance and control systems. In the summer of 1943, Hitler ordered the manufacture of rockets and flying bombs in tens of thousands but technical difficulties in development, combined with British bombing of the research station on the night of 17–18 August 1943, postponed the introduction of V-weapons until the summer and autumn of 1944. The rockets were taken under the control of Heinrich Himmler's SS construction agency, which set up a notorious underground facility at Nordhausen known as Mittelbau Dora; thousands of camp prisoners died in its construction and operation. The Fieseler flying bomb was easier to produce and it came into operation in the summer of 1944 when, on 13 June, the first bombs were launched against London.

British intelligence had already identified the potential threat of new weapons and from December 1943 bomber forces based in Britain were ordered to attack the weapons' production facilities and launch sites in an operation codenamed "Crossbow". The campaign reached its height during the period June to September 1944, when 74,000 tons of bombs were dropped on V-1 targets. "Crossbow" succeeded in disrupting the V-weapons programme but not in halting it. Over 10,000 flying bombs were directed at London and a number of other British cities, but only 7,488 reached England and of these only 2,419 reached London. The death toll of 6,184 was nevertheless high in proportion to the tonnage of explosive and a more effective flying-bomb campaign might well have provoked a crisis in the capital. From October 1944 the V-1 was also directed at the Belgian port of Antwerp, which was a major supply base for Allied armies.

A high proportion of V-1s were shot down by aircraft or anti-aircraft fire before they reached their target, while misinformation fed from

8 MARCH 1944
First successful trial launch of the German Wasserfall remote-controlled ground-to-air missile at Peenemünde. The anti-aircraft rocket failed to see service.

17 JULY 1944
US forces use Napalm in attacks for the first time in Europe on German troops in Normandy.

28 JULY 1944
The Messerschmitt 163B rocket-powered fighter sees combat for the first time.

4 AUGUST 1944
The British Gloster Meteor jet fighter reports first successful shooting-down of V-1 missiles.

WERNHER VON BRAUN
(1912—77)

Wernher von Braun was the most well-known rocket scientist of his generation. His teenage enthusiasm for rocketry led him to a position with the German army at the age of only 20, when he joined a research team working on ballistic missiles. He became technical director of the Army Ordnance Office in 1937 and continued his research on rocket propulsion at the Peenemünde research station set up on the Baltic coast. He led the team that developed the V-2 rocket (first used in September 1944), and in 1945 surrendered to the Americans, along with a cohort of German rocket scientists, plans and equipment. He was recruited to develop missiles for the US Army, including the Jupiter rocket. In 1960, he was transferred to NASA, where he became director of the Space Flight Center and the mastermind behind the Saturn V rocket that took the first men to the moon. He retired in 1972 to work for private industry.

OPPOSITE An infra-red image of a German V-1 launch site taken with a 30 centimetre (12-inch) lens from 300 metres (1,000 feet) on 2 December 1944. The air campaign against the V-weapons, codenamed "Crossbow", saw 60,000 tons of bombs dropped between June and September 1944, by which time many of the original sites had been overrun.

MAJOR GENERAL WALTER DORNBERGER
(1895–1980)

An artillery officer in the First World War, Walter Dornberger studied engineering during the 1920s before joining the ballistics department of the German Army Ordnance Office in April 1930. In May 1937, Dornberger, now a colonel, was put in charge of the weapons development centre at Peenemünde, where he oversaw the development of von Braun's V-2 rocket. He was also charged in 1942 with the development of the V-1 flying bomb and in December 1944 with the work on anti-aircraft missile technology. He was among the group of rocket scientists who surrendered to American soldiers in an Austrian village in May 1945 and he subsequently worked for the US Army under the Operation "Paperclip" scheme (which arranged the transfer of captured German scientists to the US). In 1950 he transferred to work for the Bell Aircraft Corporation; he retired in 1965.

OPPOSITE A British policeman comforts a survivor of a V-1 attack near Gipsy Hill in London in 1944. The missile destroyed a street of houses, killing the man's wife and wrecking his house. Almost 9,000 people were killed in the V-weapons campaign.

RIGHT The test launch of a V-2 weapon, the A-4 rocket, from the SS troop training area near Krakow in Poland in 1944. The weapons were large and complex pieces of engineering but carried a warhead of just over 900 kilograms (2,000 pounds) in weight, a fraction of the payload carried by a single Allied bomber. However, the rocket's high speed gave the warhead added impact when it struck the ground.

double-agents in Britain led the Germans to believe that their missiles were going too far north. The trajectory was readjusted and as a result many fell short of London on rural areas of the southeast.

Against the A-4 rocket there was less security. The first missile was fired on 8 September 1944. It was by its nature an imprecise weapon and the 517 rockets that hit London did so in no predictable pattern, causing the deaths of a further 2,754 civilians. The rocket was fired from small easily concealed silos and was difficult to attack from the air. Once in flight, only technical malfunction would prevent its arrival at its destination. Of the 6,000 V-2s produced, only 1,054 rockets hit England between 8 September and 27 March 1945; a further 900 were directed at Antwerp in the last months of 1944. Hitler's plan to produce the weapons in tens of thousands was frustrated by the collapse of the German war economy, fatally damaged by the impact of Allied heavy bombing.

As well as the V-1 and V-2, other weapons were developed, but they failed to see service. The V-3 long-range gun, designed to fire special shells a distance of almost 160 kilometres (100 miles), was developed in 1943 and 1944 but had to be abandoned when bombers hit the two designated sites near Calais in November 1943 and July 1944. A further weapon, the so-called V-4, was a ground-to-air missile codenamed "Wasserfall" (waterfall) which was close to mass-production in 1944 but lacked the support of Hitler in the struggle for scarce resources. The ground-to-air rocket might well have played a vital role in the war against Allied bombers but the V-1 and V-2 did nothing to dent the combined bomber offensive.

15 JUNE—10 AUGUST 1944

THE MARIANAS:
DEFENCE TO THE DEATH

After the island-hopping attacks on the Gilbert and Marshall Islands in the Central Pacific, Admiral Nimitz, Commander-in-Chief Pacific Ocean Areas, determined to capture the Marianas, a group of islands including Saipan and Guam, which were within air radius of the Japanese home islands for attacks by the new Boeing B-29 heavy bomber. Air attacks began on the island defences in February 1944, and in early June, Vice Admiral Spruance's 5th Fleet, with a grand total of 530 ships, arrived in the seas off Saipan to undertake a massive bombardment of Lieutenant General Yoshitsugu Saito's Japanese forces, whose estimated 32,000 soldiers were dug in to resist the American invasion to the last man.

An American battleship bombards the Japanese-held island of Guam on 20 July 1944, one day before the invasion. The bombardment by ships and aircraft was the heaviest and most co-ordinated of the Pacific War, leaving the Japanese garrison in a stunned state when the first wave of American marines reached the beaches.

On 15 June, elements of Lieutenant General Holland Smith's V Amphibious Corps, the 2nd and 4th Marine Divisions, attacked the southwestern beaches of Saipan through dangerous reefs and on beaches overlooked by high ground from which Japanese artillery could send a destructive barrage. Saito planned to contain the beachhead and then destroy it, but a steady flow of American reinforcements produced a breakout by day three and the seizure of Aslito airfield. Progress thereafter was slow against suicidal Japanese resistance and an operation planned for three days took three weeks to complete. On the night of 6–7 July the remains of the Japanese garrison in the north of the island undertook the largest *banzai* charge of the war. On 9 July, when the overall US commander Admiral Turner announced that Saipan was officially secured, Japanese soldiers and civilians leapt to their deaths from Marpi Point at the far northern tip of the island. The US forces suffered 3,500 dead but only 2,000 from the 32,000 of Saito's force were taken prisoner.

Two weeks later, on 21 July, Major General Roy Geiger's 3rd Amphibious Corps began the assault on Guam, an island ceded to the United States by Spain in 1898, which had been occupied by the Japanese Navy at the start of the Pacific War. The island was defended by 5,500 navy troops under Captain Yutaka Sugimoto and 13,000 army soldiers commanded by Lieutenant General Takeshi Takashima. They were dug in to prepared positions in the rugged mountainous district of the island around Mount Alifan. The beach landings on the west coast of Guam were less costly than on Saipan, though difficult to negotiate because of carefully constructed obstacles, but there followed a week of fierce fighting in which Japanese troops engaged in regular *banzai* charges, knowing full well that there was no prospect of reinforcement or fresh supplies. The island was finally secured by 10 August at the cost of a further 1,744 American dead. Only a handful of the Japanese garrison survived, retreating into the jungle areas where the last one surrendered in 1972.

While Guam was under attack, a further American assault was made on the smaller island of Tinian, five kilometres (three miles) south of Saipan, by 15,000 men of the 4th Marine Division. The island was secured by 1 August, by which time American engineers (the famous Construction Battalions or "See-Bees") had already begun to construct the first B-29 airfields. The battles for all three islands had been very costly to both sides, but Japanese resistance in defence of the outer perimeter of the home island area was now almost entirely suicidal. The fall of Saipan was greeted with dismay in Tokyo and the Japanese prime minister, General Hideki Tojo, was forced to resign from all his military and administrative positions, to be succeeded by Lieutenant General Kuniaki Koiso. The fierce defence of the Marianas made it clear that even if the defeat of Japan was now inevitable, the invasion of the heart of the Japanese Empire was likely to exact a heavy, perhaps insupportable toll on the American forces involved.

LIEUTENANT GENERAL HOLLAND "HOWLIN' MAD" SMITH
(1882–1967)

Holland Smith is generally regarded as the father of United States amphibious warfare. He joined the marines in 1905 and saw service in the Philippines (where he won the nickname "Howlin' Mad") and later in the First World War in France in 1917–18. He remained a marine officer after the war and by 1937 was in charge of operations and training at Marine Corps headquarters. In 1941, he became the first commander of the US 1st Marine Division, and in June that year was chosen to train the first dedicated amphibious warfare divisions. In August 1942, he took command of the Amphibious Corps, Pacific Fleet, which became the V Amphibious Corps for the operations against the Gilbert and Mariana islands. He commanded the expeditionary troops for the invasion of Iwo Jima before returning to the United States in July 1945 to take over the Marine Training and Replacement Camp. He retired in May 1946 and died after a long illness in 1967.

15 JUNE 1944
US B-29 bombers attack the Japanese home island of Kyushu from Chinese bases.

22/23 JUNE 1944
Red Army begins Operation "Bagration" against Army Group Centre in Belorussia.

1 AUGUST 1944
First Soviet troops carve out a small bridgehead over the River Vistula.

4 AUGUST 1944
German armies pull back from Florence to man the Gothic Line in Italy.

15 AUGUST 1944
Allied Operation "Dragoon" mounted against occupied southern France.

LIEUTENANT GENERAL YOSHITSUGU SAITO
(1890–1944)

A career cavalryman who saw his first service as a very young soldier in the last stage of the Russo-Japanese war of 1904–5, Saito rose to the rank of major general in the Kwantung army in China as chief of cavalry operations. In April 1944, he was appointed to command the Japanese Army's 43rd Division which was moving to Saipan. He became overall commander of the island's forces and organized the final *banzai* charge against the US forces on 7 July, determined that everyone should die rather than surrender an island so close to the Japanese homeland. On 10 July, he committed hara-kiri and was given a final bullet by his adjutant.

ABOVE US landing craft on the approach to the beaches on the west coast of Guam, 21 July 1944. The 3rd Marine Division and the Provisional Marine Brigade landed in two separate areas strongly supported by the ships and aircraft of Task Force 58. A destroyer can be seen in the distance.

OPPOSITE A tiny Japanese baby is carried down a mountainside on Saipan to a waiting ambulance jeep by a US marine. The baby was the only survivor found in an area of Saipan where Japanese resistance was being cleared. Many Japanese civilians committed suicide rather than fall into American hands.

22 JUNE–19 AUGUST 1944
OPERATION "BAGRATION"

On the Eastern Front the success of the operations in the Ukraine in 1943 and early 1944 had left a large German salient, held by Army Group Centre under Field Marshal Busch, around the Belorussian capital of Minsk. Here was to be found the largest concentration of German forces, and it was the defeat of Army Group Centre that became the Soviet priority for the summer of 1944.

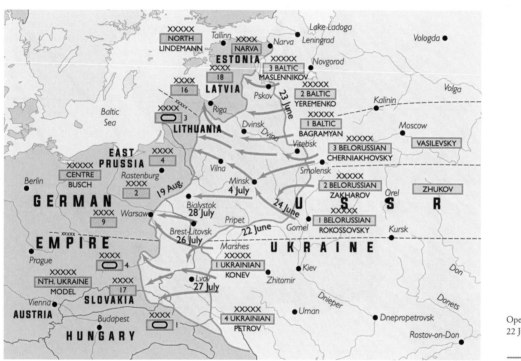

Operation Bagration,
22 June–19 August 1944

——— front lines, with date

The plans were drawn up in great secrecy between March and May and with Stalin's agreement a series of five rolling offensives were planned: from the north of the front against Finland, designed as a feint to mislead the Germans; followed by two offensives towards Minsk by the 1st and the newly created 2nd and 3rd Belorussian army groups; then a heavy attack by Marshal Ivan Konev's 1st Ukrainian army group towards the Polish city of Lvov; and finally a blow in the far south towards the Romanian oilfields. In order to mislead the Germans, who expected a continuation of the attacks in the south, a whole deception operation was mounted with dummy tanks and bases and a simulated air defence system on the southern Ukrainian part of the front. The head of German intelligence in the East, General Gehlen, told Army Group Centre to expect "a calm summer". As a result of the deception, Busch found many of his tanks and much of his artillery transferred north or south against the anticipated summer offensives.

Stalin knew the summer offensive – which he codenamed "Bagration" after a fellow Georgian and hero of the war against Napoleon – would coincide with the Allied invasion in the West, which was expected to contribute to German problems of reinforcement and priority. The date for the main assault was fixed for 19–20 June, but problems of tank supply

A group of Russian partisans crossing a river in western Belorussia in 1944. By the time of Operation "Bagration" the guerrilla movement had more than 200,000 fighters, interrupting German communications and supplies in accordance with instructions from Moscow.

FIELD MARSHAL ERNST BUSCH
(1885–1945)

Busch joined the Prussian Army in 1904 and served with distinction during the First World War. He remained in the army after the war and was made inspector of transport troops in 1925. He led the German 16th Army during the invasion of France and in the invasion of the Soviet Union in 1941, where his defence against Soviet counter-attacks around Leningrad earned him the rank of field marshal. He commanded Army Group Centre in 1943 and 1944, but after failure to stem Operation "Bagration", he was sacked by Hitler in June. He was recalled to command Army Group Northwest in March 1945 to try to stem the British attack in northern Germany, and surrendered to Montgomery on 4 May 1945. He died in a British POW camp at Aldershot in July 1945.

held up the launch until the anniversary of the German attack, 22/23 June. The first offensive against the Finns began on 10 June to distract the German defence. Then, on the night of 19–20 June, partisans began the systematic destruction of transport targets, and two days later the Soviet air force launched a fierce bombardment of German positions and air bases in Belorussia. On 23 June, part of the assault was launched with 2.4 million men, 31,000 guns, 5,200 tanks and self-propelled guns and 5,300 aircraft against the 1.2 million men, 9,500 guns, 900 tanks and 1,350 aircraft along the German central and northern front.

The element of surprise unhinged the German front. The attacks towards Minsk were spearheaded by special plough tanks to move the minefields, with infantry and tanks behind them, and searchlights used to dazzle the German defenders. On 24 June, Marshal Rokossovsky's 1st Belorussian army group, concealed at the edge of the Pripet Marshes, began a movement to encircle German forces from the south. In a week the German front collapsed, and the German 4th and 9th Armies and the 1st Panzer Army had been almost annihilated. On 28 June, Busch was replaced by Field Marshal Walter Model, regarded by Hitler as a trouble-shooting leader, but although he organized a more stable fighting retreat, by 4 July Minsk was captured and small pockets of German resistance, bypassed by the mobile Red Army, were subdued. The contrast with the slow progress of Western forces in Normandy was complete.

Over the following weeks the rolling offensives continued. The 1st Belorussian army group moved towards Warsaw, while the 2nd and

3rd Belorussian army groups moved north towards the Baltic states and East Prussia. Further south, unable now to mount an effective defence, German armies fell back before Konev's 1st Ukrainian army group. Brest-Litovsk fell on 26 July; Lvov, a day later. By 29 August, after two months of gruelling fighting, the Red Army had cleared the Germans from Belorussia, southern Poland and part of the Baltic states, capturing over 200,000 German soldiers and destroying Army Group Centre. Soviet losses – dead, missing and POWs – amounted to 179,000, but German losses between June and August in the east amounted to a remarkable 589,000. On 17 July, captured Germans, including no fewer than 19 generals, were paraded through Moscow. "Bagration" was the largest defeat ever inflicted on German armed forces.

15 JUNE 1944
Strategic air offensive against Japan begins with attacks from Chinese bases.

18 JUNE 1944
Japanese army captures city of Changsha in southern China.

25 JULY 1944
Operation "Cobra" launched in Normandy to break out from the bridgehead.

21 AUGUST 1944
Dumbarton Oaks meeting in the United States paves the way for the formation of United Nations Organization.

25 AUGUST 1944
Romania changes sides and declares war on Germany.

30 AUGUST 1944
Red Army occupies the Romanian oilfields at Ploesti, cutting Germany off from one of its main oil supplies.

MARSHAL KONSTANTIN ROKOSSOVSKY
(1896–1968)

Widely regarded as the best of the Red Army marshals during the Second World War, Rokossovsky led an adventurous and dangerous life. Born to Polish parents in the Russian-controlled area of Poland, he served in one of the premier Tsarist dragoon regiments during the First World War, first as a private, but ending the war as a commander. He joined the Red Army in 1917 and led a cavalry squadron in the Civil War, during which he was twice wounded. He became a cavalry commander in the 1920s and 1930s, rising to the rank of colonel before, as part of the purging of the Red Army, he was arrested in August 1937 on charges of sabotage and spying. Despite torture, he refused to be broken and was given only a three-year sentence. In March 1940, he was rehabilitated into the army. By June, he was a major general in command of the 5th Cavalry Corps and in October 1940 the newly formed 9th Mechanized Corps, which fought against the German invasion in the Ukraine. Rokossovsky played a key role in the defence of Moscow and later of Stalingrad. At Kursk, he was responsible for organizing the deep defensive system around the salient. He led the 1st Belorussian Front against Army Group Centre in summer 1944 and the 2nd Belorussian Front against East Prussia in 1945. He was appointed Commander-in-Chief of Soviet troops in Poland from 1945 until 1949, when he was appointed Polish defence minister and made a Polish national. In 1956, he was brought back to the Soviet Union, where he held a number of senior posts before retiring in 1962.

LEFT A group of Red Army infantry, part of the 2nd Belorussian army group, leap out of a trench in the operations in Belorussia in August 1944 in pursuit of the retreating German Army Group Centre.

25 JULY–25 AUGUST 1944

BREAKOUT: OPERATION "COBRA"

The slow progress made in the Normandy campaign in June and early July was dramatically reversed when, on 25 July 1944, the US First Army under Lieutenant General Bradley began Operation "Cobra", designed to create the conditions for a final breakout from the Normandy bridgehead into France. The original plan was for a sharp blow against the German line around St Lô with a strong force of aircraft and tanks, but the German army was so drained after 45 days of continuous combat and air attack that when "Cobra" was launched the line quickly collapsed.

Bradley had at his disposal 15 fully equipped divisions with four in reserve and an overwhelming number of tanks and aircraft. The German 7th Army had only nine weakened divisions, including the armoured Panzer Lehr Division, and 110 tanks. An air attack by heavy bombers on 24 July almost disrupted the Allied plan when aircraft hit the forward American units in error, but on 25 July "Cobra" started with

a pulverizing attack by 1,500 heavy bombers on the unfortunate Panzer Lehr Division. Resistance rapidly crumbled and instead of a preparatory forward move, Bradley found his forces racing towards the Brittany coast and the open country beyond. The speed of the attack was made possible by the development of the "Rhinoceros Tank", a Sherman tank with large steel teeth welded to the front to allow it to cut through and remove

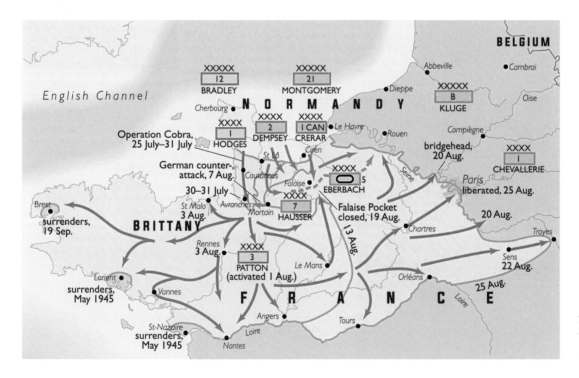

Northern France,
25 July–25 August 1944

——— front lines, with date

the thick hedgerows that made progress otherwise so slow. German forces were compelled to fight in the narrow roads, but the US forces could now deploy at speed across country.

On 28 July, the US 8th Corps reached Coutances, near the Atlantic coast, while the 4th Armored Division raced through a gap in the line to seize the town of Avranches on 30–31 July and open the way to the occupation of Brittany. Montgomery, whose British and Canadian forces were still pinned down around Caen, saw the opportunity to turn the German line and ordered Bradley to use light forces to occupy Brittany, while taking the bulk of his army eastwards to encircle von Kluge's whole army group. On 1 August, Bradley became commander-in-chief of the newly formed 12th Army Group, leaving Lieutenant General Hodges in command of 1st Army and bringing in General George Patton as commander of the new US Third Army. Patton, who had been chafing at the bit in Britain, needed no second chance. He drove his forces forward towards Le Mans and Chartres, with Paris now a distant prize. The German 7th Army and 4th Panzer Army faced the imminent prospect of complete encirclement and von Kluge asked to be allowed to retreat.

COLONEL GENERAL JOSEF "SEPP" DIETRICH
(1892–1966)

"Sepp" Dietrich, a senior Waffen-SS officer, became notorious for the so-called Malmédy massacre of American POWs in 1944. He volunteered for the Bavarian army in 1914 and became one of the first members of a German panzer unit in 1918. He fought in the postwar Freikorps and was one of the participants in the Hitler Putsch in 1923. He joined the party in 1928 and the SS the same year, becoming a parliamentary deputy in 1930. He rose rapidly through the SS ranks and in 1933 took over responsibility for guarding Hitler. During the war he led the newly formed Waffen-SS (armed SS) division "*Leibstandarte*" and later became commander of the 1st SS Panzer Corps and then Commander-in-Chief of the 6th SS Panzer Army. He served in Normandy against the Allied breakout, and again in the Ardennes offensive in December 1944. In 1946, he was tried for the murder of 70 US servicemen and sentenced to life imprisonment. He was released in 1955, sentenced again for his role in murdering SA leaders in June 1934, and finally freed in 1958, still a convinced enthusiast for National Socialism.

The Allied commanders pose for the camera during a conference in a French hayfield somewhere in northern France during the rapid Allied advance following Operation "Cobra". General Montgomery, centre, is flanked by Lieutenant General Hodges of the US First Army, General Crerar of the Canadian 1st Army, General Bradley, Commander of the US Twelfth Army Group and Lieutenant General Dempsey, commander of the British 2nd Army.

Hitler characteristically refused, ordering von Kluge not only to stand fast but to scrape together his remaining armoured units and to mount a counter-attack from the town of Mortain, 48 kilometres (30 miles) from the Atlantic coast, designed to cut off the thin US line at Avranches and restore the initiative. Hitler was entirely out of touch with the reality of the campaign. Against the protests of his officers, von Kluge reluctantly did what Hitler wanted, making defeat even more certain. ULTRA decrypts alerted the Allies, who prepared solid anti-tank defences and large-scale air attacks. The Mortain offensive began on 7 August under cover of night, but when the early-morning mists had cleared, air attacks destroyed the advance and Bradley counter-attacked, driving the weakened German divisions back to where they had come from. To mount the offensive, von Kluge had taken armoured divisions away from Caen, and this finally allowed Montgomery to push south to try to create a pocket which would trap the entire German force around the town of Falaise.

Hitler replaced von Kluge with Walter Model, hero of the fighting retreat in the East, but Model saw at once that the situation was hopeless.

25 JULY 1944
Hitler publishes decree authorizing Total War Mobilization.

26 JULY 1944
Roosevelt agrees to the invasion of the Philippines at a meeting in Honolulu.

1 AUGUST 1944
The Polish Home Army begins the Warsaw uprising.

12 AUGUST 1944
An oil pipeline codenamed "PLUTO" is completed across the English Channel, speeding up oil supply for the Allies.

19 AUGUST 1944
Field Marshal von Kluge commits suicide two days after he is replaced as C-in-C in the West by Walter Model.

23 AUGUST 1944
Romania announces an end to its Axis partnership and signs ceasefire with Red Army two weeks later.

The jaws of the Allied pincers were closing by the hour; Model ordered a retreat, which became a rout. Fighting a desperate rearguard action, large numbers of German soldiers escaped with all their equipment gone. Even so, 45,000 were captured when the pocket was sealed on 19 August. The defeated army fled towards the Seine, but Patton's 3rd Army had already reached the river, and made two crossings on 19–20 August, north and south of Paris. Model's force improvised their own river crossings, but on the far side he could organize only four weak divisions and 120 tanks against an Allied force of more than 40 divisions. Little now lay between the Allies and the German border.

OPPOSITE An enthusiastic French crowd greets troops of the US 30th Assault Unit as they enter the town of Granville on the French Atlantic coast on 31 July 1944 during the early stages of Operation "Cobra".

ABOVE Men from the US 20th Corps move through the battle-scarred countryside around Chartres on 17 August 1944 on the way to the first crossings of the River Seine. By this time the German army was in frantic retreat towards the German borders.

GENERAL COURTNEY HODGES
(1887–1966)

Courtney Hodges failed his officer training at the West Point Academy and joined the army as a private in 1906, but rose to officer status within three years. He served in the Philippines and Mexico, then in the army in France in 1918. His success as a soldier brought him appointment as an instructor at West Point despite his earlier failure. By 1941, he was commandant of the Infantry School, then chief of infantry. In 1942, he took over command of US 10th Corps, and was sent to Britain in March 1944 to serve under Bradley. He was deputy commander of the US First Army on D-Day, and in August became its commander. His forces reached Paris first, and also crossed the Rhine first over the Remagen bridge, finally meeting the Red Army in April 1945 at Torgau on the River Elbe. He was promoted to full general in April 1945, only the second man to have moved from private to general in the US Army.

14 AUGUST–14 SEPT 1944

THE END OF VICHY FRANCE: OPERATION "DRAGOON"

When plans for "Overlord" were being completed, in 1943 the Anglo-American Combined Chiefs-of-Staff decided that a subsidiary landing, codenamed Operation "Anvil", should be made in southern France at the same time. The decision was taken at the Cairo Conference in November 1943, but during the early months of 1944, Eisenhower insisted that it be postponed to ensure enough men and landing craft were available for D-Day, while in Italy the Allied commanders opposed the diversion of resources from an Italian campaign which threatened to descend into stalemate. Only Roosevelt remained fully committed and insisted, against Churchill's call for an alternative attack through southeastern Europe towards Austria, that the operation should take place.

Forces for what became known as Operation "Dragoon" were diverted from Italy. Under the overall control of the supreme commander in the Mediterranean, the British General Henry Maitland Wilson, the US Seventh Army under Lieutenant General Alexander Patch and the French Army B under General de Lattre de Tassigny were assigned to the operation, a total of 11 divisions, backed by large air and naval forces. They were opposed by 10 divisions of General Blaskowitz's 19th Army, but most were not stationed near the coast and only one, the 11th Panzer Division, was a first-class unit. The landings, supported by 887 warships and 1,370 landing craft, took place on 15 August 1944 and were largely unopposed. The German army began to withdraw, since prospects for serious defence were limited. French forces, renamed the 1st French Army on 19 September, took Toulon and Marseilles by 28 August, while the 6th Corps of Seventh Army, led by Major General Lucian Truscott, pursued the retreating enemy up the Rhone valley towards Alsace-Lorraine.

Progress was swift, for by 3 September Lyons was liberated, and by 10 September the city of Dijon was reached, where Patch's army met up with units of General Patton's US Third Army coming from the northwest. Much of the region was liberated by the French Forces of the Interior which tried to slow down the German retreat, but Blaskowitz succeeded in avoiding a trap and withdrew his forces to the Vosges region. On 15 September, the southern armies were brought under Eisenhower's command and formed into a 6th Army Group for the expected advance into Germany. The whole campaign had cost only 4,000 French and 2,700

LIEUTENANT GENERAL ALEXANDER "SANDY" PATCH
(1889–1945)

Better known for leading US forces in the campaign for the Pacific island of Guadalcanal, Alexander Patch was commander of forces for the invasion of southern France in August 1944. He joined the army in 1909 and served as an infantry officer in the First World War. In 1940, he was promoted to brigadier general and helped to train the expanding US army under General Marshall. He went to the south Pacific in 1942, where he formed what he called the "Americal Division" out of a number of smaller units stationed there. He led the division on Guadalcanal in October 1942, and in December took over command of all forces on the island, leading some operations himself. He was transferred to Europe, where he took over the US Seventh Army from Mark Clark. He led the army in the invasion of southern France and on into southern Germany by the end of the war. He returned to the United States in August 1945 to command the US Fourth Army but died of pneumonia three months later.

OPPOSITE The British prime minister, Winston Churchill, aboard the destroyer HMS *Kimberley* watching the Allied invasion of southern France on 15 August 1944. So fierce was the bombardment of the coast that the German guns were soon silenced. Churchill found the invasion as a result "rather dull".

BELOW Allied troops and self-propelled guns from the US Seventh Army land on the southern coast of France on 15 August 1944 somewhere between Toulon and Cannes in the early stages of Operation "Dragoon". The beach landings were lightly opposed after 126 warships and 2,000 aircraft had pounded the defences.

17 AUGUST 1944
Red Army reaches the old German border of East Prussia.

23 AUGUST 1944
Coup in Romania overthrows pro-Axis Marshal Antonescu.

4 SEPTEMBER 1944
British and Canadian armies capture Antwerp and secure a major port for future operations.

19 SEPTEMBER 1944
Moscow armistice signed, ending the "Continuation War" between Finland and the Soviet Union.

21 SEPTEMBER 1944
British 8th Army breaks through the Gothic Line in northern Italy.

12 SEPTEMBER 1944
"Octagon" conference convenes in Canadian city of Quebec to discuss Western strategy.

Paratroopers dropped from the C-47 transport aircraft of the 12th Air Force Troop Carrier Air Division on 15 August 1944. The troops of the 1st Airborne Task Force were dropped early in the morning west of Cannes to support the beach invasion.

American casualties, while 57,000 Germans were captured, more than the number ensnared in the Falaise pocket by Montgomery in August. Eisenhower now had a major port in Marseilles which could be used to bring in supplies and men for the next stage of the campaign to enter and occupy the German homeland.

The invasion of southern France hastened the end of the Vichy regime, which by the summer of 1944 was dominated by pro-German French Fascists under the premiership of Pierre Laval. On 19 August, the head of the Vichy regime, Marshal Pétain, resigned and was taken by the Germans first to Belfort then to Sigmaringen. In April 1945, he was allowed to leave for Switzerland, but volunteered to return to France where he stood trial and was condemned to death (later commuted to life imprisonment). Laval followed Pétain to Belfort and Sigmaringen with the remnants of the Vichy government. He was captured in July 1945, sentenced to death for treason and executed.

The government of France was now taken over by General de Gaulle's French Committee for National Liberation, which became the de facto provisional government. The Third Republic, which had been replaced by Vichy in 1940, was not reconstituted. Instead, a new republican constitution for the French Fourth Republic was agreed in 1946 following national elections in October 1945 that gave overwhelming support to the parties of the left, and to the legacy of the resistance against German occupation and the authoritarian Vichy system.

MARSHAL JEAN DE LATTRE DE TASSIGNY (1889–1952)

Jean de Lattre was descended from a Franco-Flemish aristocratic family. He joined the French army in 1908, and as a young officer in the 12th Dragoons was wounded twice in the first month of the First World War. He had become an infantry captain by the end of the war and pursued an army career in the interwar years, rising to the rank of brigadier general in March 1939, when he was chief-of-staff of the French 5th Army. He commanded the 14th Infantry Division in the Battle of France and then became a general in the Vichy French army. Arrested late in 1942 after the German occupation of the whole of France, he escaped from prison and made his way to London. He was promoted to full general by General de Gaulle and put in command of French Army B. He led the force in the landings in southern France, liberated Toulon and Marseilles, and then entered Germany in 1945 alongside the Allies. He represented France at the German surrender in Berlin in May 1945. He was created a marshal of France shortly after his death in 1952.

BELOW A Sherman tank manned by men of the Free French Army B in the port city of Marseilles on 29 August 1944 after the city had fallen to a French attack the previous day. Although Hitler had designated Marseilles and Toulon as "fortress cities" they fell quickly to determined French assault.

23–25 AUGUST 1944

THE LIBERATION OF PARIS

As Allied forces broke out of the Normandy bridgehead, the population of Paris began to prepare for their liberation. However, General Eisenhower did not initially give Paris priority, preferring to bypass the capital while Allied forces chased the German army to the German frontier. General Patton's US Third Army reached and crossed the Seine at Mantes-Gassicourt on the night of 19–20 August, some 60 kilometres (37 miles) north of Paris, and followed that with crossings south of Paris at Melun and Fontainebleau on 24 August. American forces then raced on across France in pursuit of around 250,000 German soldiers retreating towards the German frontier.

The Allied assumption was that the Germans would abandon Paris, and they detailed General Leclerc's 2nd Armoured Division as the unit with the honour of entering the city first when it was finally free of German forces. The population of Paris reacted to the news of the American advance by starting the liberation of their capital themselves. The starting point was a strike movement, beginning with railway workers on 10 August but followed, when news came of the Allied landings in the south, by a large part of the Paris police force on 15 August. The liberation movement in Paris was divided between the Gaullists and the Communists, led by Henri Tanguy, who was head of the local Committee of Liberation, but on 19 August, following a call for general mobilization by the French Forces of the Interior the day before, the two groups finally worked together when they launched a rising in the city against the German garrison commanded by General Dietrich von Choltitz.

There was still an element of risk in mounting a rising, for at the same time German forces were brutally suppressing a similar revolt in Warsaw. Hitler, who had visited Paris in June 1940 and respected it as a centre of architectural splendour, now ordered Choltitz to defend Paris at all costs and to destroy what could not be defended. All over the city sporadic fighting broke out, while in the main communist districts barricades were set up. The Gaullist leader, Alexandre Parodi, tried with the help of the Swedish consul-general to calm the fighting down. What followed were six days of confusion until Choltitz, a Prussian officer of the old school rather than a National Socialist fanatic, finally decided to ignore Hitler's orders

OPPOSITE During the liberation of Paris in August 1944 two soldiers from the 2nd French Armoured Division in the shadow of the Arc de Triomphe fire at German snipers and French Milice trying to rescue German prisoners, who lie dead on the Champs-Elysées.

OVERLEAF French resistance fighters behind a makeshift barricade in Paris with an assortment of weapons and helmets. The rising against the German garrison began on 19 August and lasted until the city was liberated by Allied armies six days later.

3 JULY 1944
Belorussian capital of Minsk liberated by Red Army.

24 JULY 1944
Polish city of Lublin liberated by the advancing Soviet forces.

1 AUGUST 1944
Polish Home Army begins uprising to liberate the city before the arrival of the Red Army.

9 AUGUST 1944
Officials in Algiers announce formal end to the Vichy regime.

26 AUGUST 1944
French southern port of Toulon liberated during Operation "Dragoon".

29 AUGUST 1944
Slovak uprising begins against German occupying forces.

GENERAL JACQUES-PHILIPPE LECLERC DE HAUTECLOQUE (1902–47)

Philippe, Count of Hautecloque, changed his name in 1945 to Jacques-Philippe Leclerc in order to incorporate his wartime resistance alias. He graduated from the Saint-Cyr military academy in 1924, and was an army captain by 1937. After the defeat of France in June 1940, he went to London and joined de Gaulle's Free French army. He saw service in West and North Africa before joining in the Normandy invasion with the French 2nd Armoured Division. He was allowed to enter Paris to liberate the city, and then led his unit to liberate Strasbourg. His forces ended the  war at Hitler's Bavarian residence at Berchtesgaden. He then commanded French forces in Indo-China (Vietnam) in the civil war there in 1945, but was replaced because he favoured negotiation. He died in a plane crash in 1947, and was awarded the posthumous rank of marshal of France in 1952.

LEFT The German commander in Paris, General Dietrich von Choltitz, signs the act of surrender on 25 August 1944. Though ordered by Hitler to leave nothing in Paris standing, Choltitz had no desire to be remembered as the man who destroyed the capital.

BELOW General de Gaulle, leader of the Free French, and soon to be head of a provisional French administration, walks from the Arc de Triomphe down the Champs-Elysées to the cathedral of Notre Dame, where a service of thanksgiving was to take place on 26 August 1944. In the cathedral a sniper fired at de Gaulle. Sporadic fighting continued for some days.

OPPOSITE Overjoyed Parisians greet a tank of the French 2nd Armoured Division commanded by General Leclerc as it arrives at Place Michel-Ange-Auteuil on 24 August 1944.

and surrender. On 23 August, Eisenhower had given permission for Leclerc to leave pursuit of the German army temporarily and to secure Paris. The first French armoured columns reached central Paris on the evening of 24 August and the following day the whole of the capital was liberated amidst scenes of wild celebration. Some 3,200 Germans were killed in the rising and 1,500 French; a further 12,800 German soldiers were taken prisoner.

On 26 August, General de Gaulle entered Paris in triumph. He rekindled the flame on the tomb of the unknown warrior at the Arc de Triomphe and then marched at the head of Allied forces down the Champs-Elysées. He later went to Notre Dame, where he was shot at by a sniper concealed in the cathedral. That evening the German air force made a final retributive attack on Paris, the heaviest raid of the war. Around 500 houses were destroyed and the huge wine warehouse the Halle aux Vins was set on fire, illuminating the whole of central Paris.

The experience of Paris was not universal in France. Around 85 per cent of French communes waited for the arrival of Allied forces and did not risk German revenge. The liberation of Paris was a necessary and symbolic act, which was why de Gaulle chose it as the site for his first major speech on French soil when he talked of a city that had "liberated itself" in order to liberate France. The Committee for National Liberation moved from Algiers to Paris and set about reconstituting a unitary and democratic country.

HENRI ROL-TANGUY
(1908–2002)

Henri Tanguy was a French communist who became commander of the resistance French Forces of the Interior in Paris in June 1944. He was the son of a sailor who became an active Young Communist in Paris in the 1920s and 1930s. In 1937, he joined the International Brigades fighting against Franco's uprising in Spain and was wounded at the Battle of Ebro. He went underground after French defeat in 1940. Under the pseudonym "Colonel Rol" he organized the resistance group Francs-Tireurs et Partisans in Paris. He was one of the leaders of the uprising in the city in August 1944. He joined the French 1st Army fighting its way into Germany and then remained a regular army officer until 1962. He became a member of the French Communist Party central committee, on which he served until 1987. He was made an honorary Spanish citizen in 1996 for his role in the Spanish Civil War.

17–26 SEPTEMBER 1944

OPERATION "MARKET GARDEN": ARNHEM

The sudden collapse of German resistance in France in August 1944 opened up the prospect that the war in the West might be brought to a rapid conclusion if Allied armies could penetrate into Germany fast enough. Montgomery's 21st Army Group and Bradley's 12th Army Group pushed on into eastern France and Belgium during September. On 4 September, the port of Antwerp was captured, but not the Scheldt estuary to the north, which was still defended by scattered German units, making it impossible to use the major port for supplying Allied armies. The sheer speed of the advance had produced a crisis of supply which threatened to undermine the ambition to destroy German resistance by the winter.

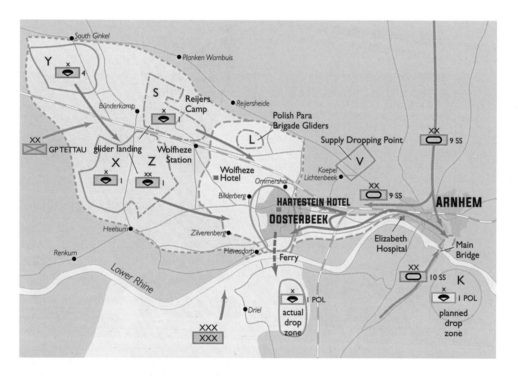

Arnhem, 17–26 September 1944

```
----    front line, 17 September
- - -   front line, 21 September
─────   final perimeter, 26 September
═════   Allied drop/landing zone
```

It was in this strategic context that Montgomery now suggested a daring operation to try to accelerate the Allied advance. "Market Garden" was designed to drive a salient into the German line towards the Dutch city of Arnhem, force a crossing of the lower Rhine and create the conditions for Allied forces to sweep down towards the industrial region of the Ruhr.

It was an ambitious plan, and left the estuary around Antwerp still in enemy hands, but on 10 September Eisenhower approved it and agreed to make available the First Allied Airborne Army led by US Lieutenant General Lewis Brereton, but under the tactical command of the British Lieutenant General Frederick Browning. The three airborne divisions

ABOVE An aerial view of Airspeed Horsa and GAL Hamilcar gliders on Landing Zone "Z" near Wolfheze woods, northwest of the Dutch city of Arnhem on 17 September 1944. Operation "Market Garden" depended on the successful transport of airborne forces and equipment, including the operation's headquarters staff and commander.

15 SEPTEMBER 1944

US marines land on the island of Peleliu meeting fierce resistance.

16 SEPTEMBER 1944

Bulgarian capital of Sofia falls under Soviet control.

18 SEPTEMBER 1944

British and US aircraft drop supplies to the Polish Home Army in Warsaw.

25 SEPTEMBER 1944

Hitler announces formation of the *Volkssturm* volunteer movement of German men from 16 to 60 to resist the Allied advance into Germany.

14 SEPTEMBER 1944

Red Army begins operations towards the Yugoslav capital of Belgrade.

US forces make the first breach in the German Siegfried Line near Aachen.

were allocated different tasks. The US 82nd and 101st Divisions were to seize the Nijmegen and Eindhoven bridges over the River Waal and the Wilhelmina canal, while the British 1st Airborne Division was to capture the bridges at Arnhem and create a narrow bridgehead across the Rhine. While the airborne forces fought for the bridges, Lieutenant General Horrocks was to bring his 30th Corps forward through the narrow passageway carved out of the German line to strengthen the Allied grip on Arnhem.

The operation began on 17 September with mixed fortunes. The 19,000 troops were dropped into the combat zones more accurately than was often the case, but the attempt to cross eight water barriers was in itself a challenge. Browning insisted on taking part in the operation personally, taking the whole headquarters staff by glider to Arnhem, but he found it difficult to hold together the scattered airborne units with poor radio communications. The American divisions succeeded in taking their objectives in Eindhoven and Nijmegen, but further north

LIEUTENANT GENERAL FREDERICK BROWNING
(1896–1965)

Generally regarded as the father of the British airborne forces, Frederick Browning began his career in the First World War with the Grenadier Guards. He was a Guards commander in the early years of the Second World War until appointed in November 1941 to command the British 1st Airborne Division. He designed the distinctive maroon beret for the force and played a key part in their organization and training. In April 1943, he became airborne advisor to Eisenhower in the Mediterranean theatre, where he helped to plan the Sicily invasion, and in December 1943 was commander of Headquarters Airborne Troops under Montgomery. After the Normandy invasion, he became deputy commander of the 1st Allied Airborne Army and in this capacity helped to organize and lead Operation "Market Garden". After its failure he was sent as chief-of-staff to the Southeast Asia Command. After the war, he became comptroller of the Royal Household.

the 1st Airborne Division met stiff German resistance and failed to take the bridges over the Rhine. The 9th and 10th SS Panzer Divisions were refitting at Arnhem and although Browning had been warned by his intelligence officers that the divisions had been detected, he chose to launch the operation regardless. The result was strong German counter-attacks in and around Arnhem that forced the British 2nd Parachute Battalion to surrender on 21 September. The expected help from the 30th Corps did not materialize. Horrocks's units were held up by the slow process of bridge-building and by bad weather and reached the River Waal only on 21 September. They crossed it the following day, only to find that the British position was now hopeless. Airborne forces were ordered to make their way back across the Waal on 25 September and the operation was abandoned.

Montgomery's gamble failed to pay off and involved a heavy cost. The 1st Airborne Division suffered 7,842 casualties, including 6,000 prisoners. The two American divisions, which held the salient they had formed for a further two months, suffered total casualties of 3,532. Browning

LIEUTENANT GENERAL BRIAN HORROCKS
(1895–1985)

Brian Horrocks was one of the most popular and well-regarded British generals of the Second World War whose long army career was spiced with incident. He almost failed his cadet course at Sandhurst, but the outbreak of the First World War gave him the opportunity to prove himself in battle. He was wounded and captured in October 1914 and spent four years trying to escape; in exasperation the Germans put him in a Russian POW camp, where he learnt fluent Russian. On repatriation in 1919 he volunteered to serve with the British intervention in Russia, where he was captured again in January 1920 and held as a prisoner for ten months. He had become a career soldier and by the outbreak of war was an instructor at the staff college. He commanded a machine-gun battalion in France, and a division in Britain in 1941. He was sent to North Africa to command the 13th Corps under Montgomery in 1942, where his unit defended the Alam Halfa ridge in the battle in early September 1942. He played a key role in Tunisia and accepted the surrender of Rommel's Afrika Korps. In June 1943, he was severely wounded, but in August 1944 was back in command of 30th Corps which he led in Operation "Market Garden". At the end of the war he was promoted to lieutenant general and in 1949 he was appointed gentleman usher of the Black Rod in the House of Lords.

took much of the blame for the failure, but he had famously warned Montgomery early in September that Arnhem might be "a bridge too far". In October and November 1944, Montgomery concentrated instead on clearing the Scheldt estuary and freeing Antwerp as a supply base, a campaign that was only completed on 8 November with the capture of Walcheren at the mouth of the river. By late November, the port could at last be used, but Allied armies had been brought to a halt along the German frontier where months of bitter fighting still lay ahead.

OPPOSITE A German infantry battalion hunting for British troops in the suburbs of Arnhem during the battle for the river crossings in the town. German resistance was heavier than anticipated.

ABOVE A line of British paratroopers captured by the German defenders of Arnhem. After months of Allied success in Western Europe, Arnhem was a sharp reminder of the remaining fighting-power of the German enemy. Around 6,000 Allied soldiers were taken prisoner.

20 OCT 1944–14 AUGUST 1945

THE RECAPTURE OF THE PHILIPPINES

In July 1944, American commanders met in Hawaii to decide on the future course of the war against Japan. The navy favoured a direct approach to the Japanese home islands, supported by air power, while the army, represented by General MacArthur, wanted to liberate the Philippines, first to establish secure bases for further operations, and second as a point of honour to free the islands from Japanese rule. Roosevelt ruled in MacArthur's favour and in September 1944 carrier-borne aircraft began a systematic destruction of Japanese airpower on the islands.

The American planners chose the island of Leyte, in the more weakly defended central area of the islands, as the starting point for the invasion. In mid-October, 700 ships and approximately 174,000 men sailed into position. On 17 October, US Rangers landed on the smaller islands of Suluan and Dinagat to secure the approaches to Leyte Gulf. Three days later, on the morning of 20 October, four divisions landed on Leyte against minimal resistance. While a major naval battle developed in and around the landing area on 24 and 25 October, the Japanese 35th Army was pushed back and airfields were secured. The Japanese commander in the Philippines, General Tomoyuki Yamashita, the conqueror of Malaya, decided to make Leyte the point at which to contest the American campaign and 45–50,000 reinforcements were sent over the following two months. By mid-December, however, the Americans had landed some 200,000 men on the island, and organized Japanese resistance ended on 19 December with over 80,000 Japanese dead, although sporadic fighting continued for a further week.

While the grip on Leyte was consolidated, MacArthur ordered assault forces to seize the island of Mindoro as a stepping stone to the conquest of the main island of Luzon. On 15 December, Mindoro was invaded and, by the middle of January 1945, secured. On 9 January, two corps of Lieutenant General Krueger's Sixth Army landed at Lingayen Bay on the west coast of Luzon and rapidly advanced across the central plain to the capital, Manila. Yamashita decided not to contest the advance but to hold his sizeable army in the mountains, forcing the Americans to fight a protracted and costly campaign. Although the Japanese High Command had decided to abandon Luzon, and sent no further reinforcements from mid-January, the surviving garrison decided to fight to the death as had many others during the island campaign. Rear Admiral Sanji Iwabuchi

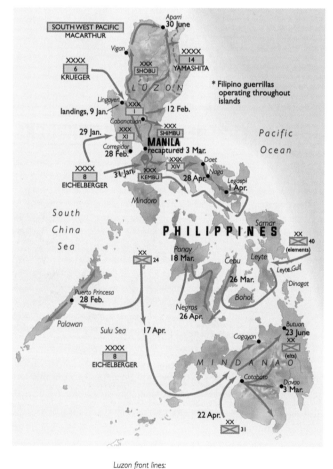

The Philippines, 1945

Luzon front lines:
——— 15 March   - - - - 20 August

10 MARCH 1945

Destruction of central Tokyo in a firestorm following heavy attack by US B-29 bombers.

3 MAY 1945

Allied forces capture Rangoon in Burma from the Japanese.

30 JUNE 1945

Japanese resistance ends on the island of Okinawa.

14 AUGUST 1945

Japanese emperor announces surrender.

retreated with a force of sailors into Manila and held out in the city between 3 February, when the Sixth Army arrived, and 3 March when the Japanese force was all but annihilated. During the siege around 100,000 Filipinos were killed by artillery fire, conflagrations and deliberate violence by the desperate Japanese forces. The battle for Manila cost US forces around 1,000 dead against 16,000 Japanese.

LIEUTENANT GENERAL WALTER KRUEGER
(1881–1967)

Walter Krueger had the distinction of being born in Germany, the son of a Prussian aristocrat, and then after emigrating with his family to the United States in 1889, to have risen through the ranks of the US Army from volunteer private to general. He first saw action in the Spanish-American war of 1898 in Cuba, then the next year went to the Philippines where he fought against the Filipino insurrection following America's overthrow of the Spanish colonial regime. He stayed in the army and was posted to France in 1918 despite French objections to his German origins. At the start of the Second World War, he was in command of the US Third Army, but in February 1943 he was posted to the southwest Pacific in command of Sixth Army, in which he founded the Alamo Scouts, whose job, like the Chindits, was to act in small groups behind enemy lines. He led the army through all the campaigns of the region and ended up occupying Japan late in 1945. He was promoted to full general when he retired in July 1946.

Ships of US Task Force 38 sail into Lingayen Gulf on the western coast of the Philippine island of Luzon shortly before the landings scheduled for 9 January. Japanese positions were subjected to a heavy and continuous bombardment. The lead ship is the battleship USS *Pennsylvania*.

While Manila was secured, US forces captured the Bataan Peninsula and the fortress of Corregidor, scene of the final American defence three years before. Before the fortress fell, Japanese forces ignited a large munitions dump, creating a colossal explosion, a fitting finale to the eclipse of Japanese power in the islands. Over the following months, some 38 separate landings to clear the southern and central islands were made by Lieutenant General Eichelberger's Eighth US Army in collaboration with Filipino guerrillas. In June, Krueger's Sixth Army was withdrawn. Over the course of the whole campaign the Japanese garrisons, some of which continued to exist in mountains and jungles until the end of the war, endured overwhelmingly high losses. In the conquest of the islands the American forces lost 13,381 killed, 48,631 wounded and over 93,000 casualties from sickness and accident.

While American forces were securing the Philippines, a less glamorous campaign was waged further to the west, as Australian troops cleared Japanese positions in Borneo and the Dutch East Indies to secure the oil supplies there, while the remaining Japanese soldiers, beyond any prospect of reinforcement or assistance, spent the rest of the war in a vicious conflict with local anti-Japanese guerrillas organized by the Special Operations Australia units infiltrated onto the island in March and April 1945. The last Japanese only surrendered in October 1945.

BELOW The port of Manila under heavy artillery bombardment on 23 February 1945 as the US Sixth Army fought for the capital. Caught in the crossfire are thought to have been around 100,000 Filipinos killed, many by the Japanese occupiers.

OPPOSITE Troops of the 9th Australian Division land from a US landing ship on the island of Labuan off the coast of the island of Borneo on 10 June 1945. Australian and Dutch forces, supported by Australian and US ships, re-occupied key areas in the East Indies in the last months of the war.

1939–1948

BEHIND BARBED WIRE: THE FATE OF POWS

Of the many millions of men and women mobilized to fight the Second World War, a substantial proportion became prisoners of the enemy. Their treatment and survival rates varied a great deal between the different combatant powers. In many cases, in contravention of the Geneva Convention, they were used as forced labour for war-related purposes. In some cases, most notably the German efforts to recruit a Russian Liberation Army from captured Red Army soldiers, prisoners became soldiers fighting against their former comrades.

The number of prisoners caught reflected the pattern of victory or defeat. Around 5.2 million Soviet soldiers were captured in the period of German victories in the east, when great encirclement operations ensnared whole Soviet armies. From 1944, it was the turn of the Soviet side to capture large numbers of Germans, while Soviet POW losses declined sharply. The British captured 600,000 Italian (including Italian colonial) soldiers in Africa, many of whom had no stomach for the contest; in Sicily, too, Italian soldiers surrendered in large numbers. German soldiers were captured in millions only in the last weeks of the war when American, British Commonwealth and French forces defeated the German army in Germany and Italy. In the Asian and Pacific wars, Japan took large numbers of prisoners in the first weeks of the war in 1941–42, but thereafter relatively few; Japanese soldiers were ordered not to surrender, and around 1.7 million Japanese soldiers, sailors and airmen died in the war, fighting suicidally rather than give in.

Once captured, the fate of prisoners was highly variable. In the war in the West both sides respected as far as they could the 1929 Geneva Convention (though on both sides there were cases where prisoners were killed on the battlefield) and camps were visited by the Red Cross. In most camps, the NCOs were responsible for keeping the discipline of their own rank and file, which in the case of some POW camps for SS soldiers in Britain led to kangaroo courts and the murder of anti-Hitler Germans. For servicemen caught in the West, there was an endless round of camp sports, entertainment, camp newspapers and journals and occasional attempts at escape. Since many Axis prisoners were sent to the United States, Canada and Australia, escape was pointless. But British and American servicemen regularly tried to escape from German prison

1929
Third Geneva Convention for protection of POWs signed. USSR and Japan failed to ratify it.

JUNE 1941
USSR asks Germany to agree to Red Cross supervision of POWs. Germany refuses.

1946–51
Far Eastern War Crimes Trials of Japanese soldiers accused of mistreatment of POWs.

1949
Fourth Geneva Convention signed.

camps and, once free, to contact underground escape organizations which could help them reach Switzerland, Sweden, Spain or Portugal. Around 35,000 escaped or evaded capture during the war. In Britain, prisoners were recruited to work on farms and building projects, and after the war, German POWs were kept back from repatriation until 1947–48, despite protests, because they provided a necessary contribution to British economic recovery.

On the Eastern Front, the prisoner regime was much harsher. Neither Germany nor the Soviet Union had been prepared for the scale of the prisoner population. Red Army soldiers were herded into makeshift enclosures in the summer and autumn of 1941 and typhus became endemic. Lack of food, shelter and sanitation decimated the prisoner population and an estimated 2.4 to 3 million died. Eventually, in response to labour shortages in Germany, Hitler agreed to allow Soviet prisoners to be transported west to work, predominantly on essential military building projects and in agriculture.

Prisoners of the Japanese were also forced to work, usually in debilitating conditions and subject to savage punishments, inflicted in part because the Japanese despised soldiers who surrendered or were captured. Captured

German POWs working in the vegetable garden at Glen Mill POW camp in Oldham, Lancashire on Christmas Eve 1940. Few German prisoners had yet been captured and not until 1942 were significant numbers in British hands.

Chinese soldiers were often murdered, and occasionally recruited to fight for the local Japanese militia.

Many POWs continued to suffer once the war was over. German soldiers died in the makeshift camps set up by the Western Allies, who simply had nowhere to house them and no plan to supply them with food. Red Army prisoners returned to the Soviet Union were all interrogated by SMERSH, the anti-spying organization set up in 1943, and many were sent to labour camps from fear that they had been contaminated by fascism. For prisoners free to return home there were ambiguous feelings provoked both by defeat and also by victory in which they had been unable to take part.

GERMAN POWS IN THE SOVIET UNION

In the early days of the German–Soviet war, only small numbers of Germans were captured by the Red Army. From Stalingrad onwards, more and more were captured, though some died on the way to prison camps or were killed when they were captured. German sources calculate that 3,155,000 German soldiers ended up in captivity, while Soviet records show only 2,730,000. There are also very wide differences in the calculation of how many prisoners died, principally from cold, hunger and disease. The German figure suggests that 1,186,000 died or were killed, while Soviet security records show only 380,000 deaths. After the war, German POWs were forced to help rebuild the shattered towns and infrastructure of the Soviet Union and were repatriated slowly to Germany, 1.4 million by 1948, and the last prisoners only in 1956, by which time they had played an important part in Soviet reconstruction.

COLDITZ CASTLE

The eleventh-century German castle at Colditz, Saxony, was used during the Second World War as a prison camp for officers who were either inveterate escapers or regarded as a security risk. The castle had been used as a mental asylum between 1829 and 1924, and during the early years of the Third Reich housed political prisoners and so-called "asocials". In 1939, designated Oflag IV-C, it became a camp for Polish and French officers, then a high-security camp for British escapers, including Wing Commander Douglas Bader. The nature of the prison population made further escape attempts inevitable. There were around 300 attempts, and 30 successful escapes. The war ended before a glider, under construction in an attic area, could be used to mount yet another escape bid.

LEFT A view of the prisoners' courtyard in the high-security POW prison at Colditz.

OPPOSITE A picture of American POWs taken in Bilibid prison in the Philippines, capital of Manila, on 8 February 1945, shortly after their liberation. Thousands of prisoners died in Japanese captivity from murder, hunger and disease.

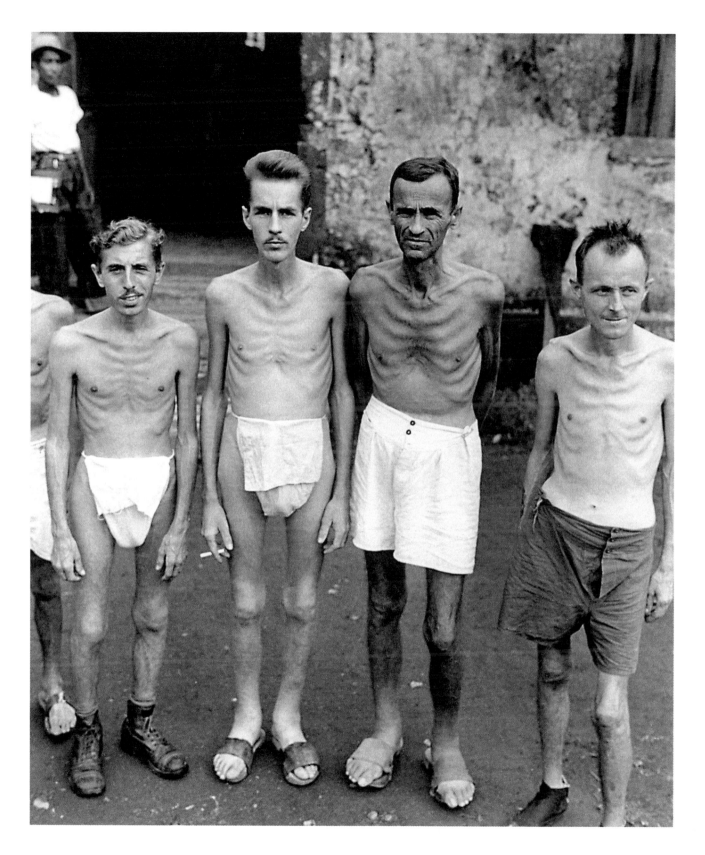

POWS IN JAPAN

Family photographs of Sergeant Ken Wyse, captured on a Chindit operation in April 1943, on the back of which colleague Flight Lieutenant J.K. Edmonds recorded Wyse's capture, subsequent mistreatment and death in a prison camp in Rangoon on 21 August 1943. Edmonds survived the war as a prisoner of the Japanese and returned the photos and wallet they were kept in to Wyse's family.

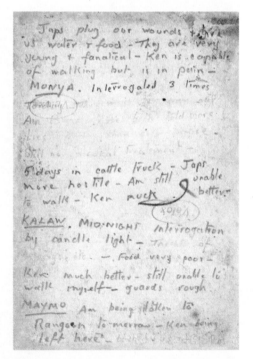

APRIL. 28

Both Ken + myself + Col Alexander Wounded — Col A. seriously wounded in thigh + bleeding badly — Ken has slight wound in hip + two bullets thru stomach.

We managed to carry Col A several hundred yards, but we were too weak to go further. Col A died —

We hid in some long grass, intending to make our get-away after dark —

Our wounds stiffened up — neither of us could walk — very thirsty — Japs are searching for us — Ken says his Mother will know that he is wounded — Japs pass within 10 ft of us — our chances look very slim — Ken appears unconcious — have no hat — sun very hot — would give anything for a drink — shots being fired near + a good deal v +

Japs plug our wounds + give us water + food — They are very young + fanatical — Ken is capable of walking but is in pain — MONYA. Interrogated 3 times

Am ...

Still no medical treatment —

5 days in cattle truck — Japs more hostile — Am still unable to walk — Ken much better —

KALAW. Midnight interrogation by candle light — ... — Food very poor —

Ken much better — still unable to walk myself — guards rough.

MAYMO Am being taken to Rangoon tomorrow — Ken being left here —

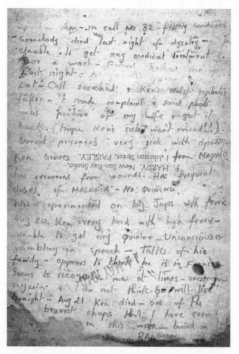

Fri – Am – in cell No 82 – filthy conditions. – Somebody died last night of dysentry – Unable to get any medical treatment – nor a wash – ... bather me up. Last night – ... ... Lot – Cell searched + Ken's Watch + photo's taken – I made complaint + said photo was picture of my wife + got it back. (hope Ken's sister won't mind!!). Several prisoners very sick with dysentry. Ken + I from MAYMO – Ken braves – 1 Johnson Street, PAISLEY, ... F. HARDY, New Sun-Ray Studio, now recovered from wounds. Has frequent doses of MALARIA – No quinine. Nips experimented on by Japs with fever. Aug 20. Ken very bad with high fever – unable to get any quinine – Unconcious & rambling in speech – Talks of his family – appears to think he is in France. Seems to recognise me at times – unconcious again + I do not think he will live tonight. – Aug 21 Ken died – one of the bravest chaps that I have seen in this war – buried in RANGOON.

Buried Ken to-day in Rangoon. Held short service, but I could not remember much of it, so had to make most of it up.

... gave us very little time. They are frightened of RAF bombers.

Hope to be out of here by Christmas. 6 have died in last 12 weeks, + many more will die unless we get more food + some medical supplies – No Red Cross. Japs very confident of Victory.

16 DECEMBER 1944–25 JANUARY 1945

BATTLE OF THE BULGE

As the Allied armies pushed towards the German frontier in September 1944, Hitler argued for a fresh campaign to try to stem the tide in the west and to divide the Western Allies, both literally, by driving a heavily armed wedge between the American and British Commonwealth armies, and psychologically, by sowing confusion and argument between them. Although his senior commanders in the west, field marshals von Rundstedt and Model, were both reluctant to undertake too ambitious an operation given Germany's weakening position, Hitler got his way by insisting on an operation that later came to be known as the Battle of the Bulge.

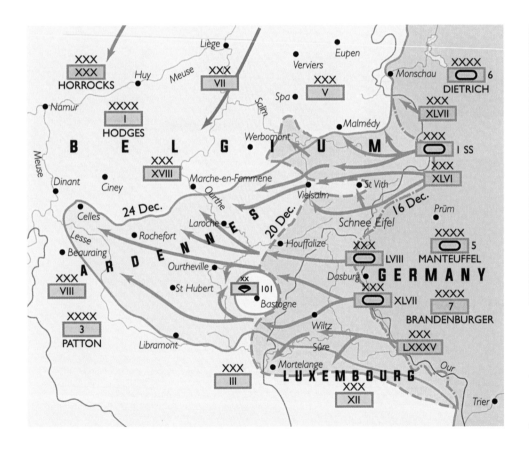

The Battle of the Bulge,
16–24 December 1944

front lines, with date

28 NOVEMBER 1944

First Allied convoy reaches Antwerp after clearing of Scheldt estuary.

31 DECEMBER 1944

Fighting finally comes to an end on the Philippine island of Leyte.

14 JANUARY 1945

Red Army offensive into East Prussia.

17 JANUARY 1945

The Polish capital of Warsaw is finally liberated from German rule.

20 JANUARY 1945

Hungarian provisional government signs armistice with the Allies.

The initial German codename for the counter-offensive was Operation "Watch on the Rhine", chosen to mislead the Allies by suggesting a defensive intention. The plan, later renamed "Autumn Mist", was to use two large Panzer armies to drive through the very same Ardennes woodland that had been exploited so successfully in the invasion of France in May 1940, with the aim of crossing the River Meuse and capturing the Allies' major supply port at Antwerp. Preparations involved the strictest secrecy and a radio silence so absolute that Allied ULTRA intelligence detected nothing of the build-up and plan. The 6th SS Panzer Army under SS General Sepp Dietrich was to spearhead the drive to Antwerp; on his

A briefing meeting at Hitler's headquarters to discuss Operation "Bodenplatte", the air support for the Ardennes offensive in December 1944. Hitler is unusually photographed wearing glasses. On his extreme right is the German air force commander-in-chief, Hermann Göring; on Hitler's far left the army chief-of-staff, General Heinz Guderian.

FIELD MARSHAL WALTER MODEL
(1891–1945)

Walter Model was one of the most successful of German field generals and a staunch supporter of the Third Reich. He joined the German army in 1909 and fought in the First World War until severely wounded in 1917, after which he held a number of staff appointments. He stayed in the army after the war, rising to the rank of colonel by 1934. He became chief of the Technical Office of the General Staff in 1935 and was promoted to major general three years later. He was chief-of-staff of the IV Corps in Poland and of the 16th Army in France and commander of the 3rd Panzer Division in the invasion of the Soviet Union. In October 1941, he became a general of Panzer troops and commander of the 41st Army Corps, and in 1942 commander of the 9th Army, which he led in the key battle of Kursk in July 1943. In 1944, he took over Army Group North in Russia and was promoted field marshal, but during Operation "Bagration" he took over Army Group Centre and stabilized the German front. Hitler regarded him as someone who could perform miracles in a difficult situation. After halting the Russian advance, he was rushed to France in August 1944 to try to prevent disaster there. He withdrew the German army to western Germany, where his Army Group B was finally overwhelmed in the Ruhr pocket in April 1945. He killed himself on 21 April 1945 in a forest near Duisburg.

left was General Hasso von Manteuffel's 5th Panzer Army, which was to cross the Meuse and swing north to the coast; both were to be protected from flank attack by General Erich Brandenberger's 7th Army to the south. A total of 500,000 men, almost 1,000 tanks and 1,000 aircraft, most of them fighters, were gathered together to strike at the weakest point of the Allied line, held by 83,000 American troops, some of them new units, some resting from fighting elsewhere.

The operation was nonetheless a gamble. Overall the Allies were much stronger and the drive to the coast carried the same risk it had run in 1940 of exposing long and vulnerable flanks to possible counter-attack. Success relied on speed, surprise and poor weather, which would limit Allied air action. On 16 December, in winter conditions too poor for air action, the German armies attacked. The front line gave way under the sheer weight of the assault, but did not crack entirely. Eisenhower sent the

US Seventh Armored Division to strengthen defences around the small Belgian town of St Vith against the 6th SS Panzer units, while the 101st Airborne arrived in Bastogne to prevent the road junction from falling easily into enemy hands. German paratroopers and a special unit, dressed in American uniforms and led by SS Lieutenant Colonel Otto Skorzeny, infiltrated Allied rear areas to cause panic and disruption, but their impact on the battle was also less than had been hoped. Those caught were shot.

The Allied response was rapid. As it became clear just how large the German assault was, Eisenhower ordered all other fighting to stop so that

ABOVE Troops from the 1st SS Panzer Division pause by a signpost to the Belgian towns of St Vith and Malmédy, scenes of some of the toughest fighting in the Battle of the Bulge. At Malmédy on 17 December 1944, 84 US prisoners were massacred by troops of SS Colonel Joachim Peiper's battle group.

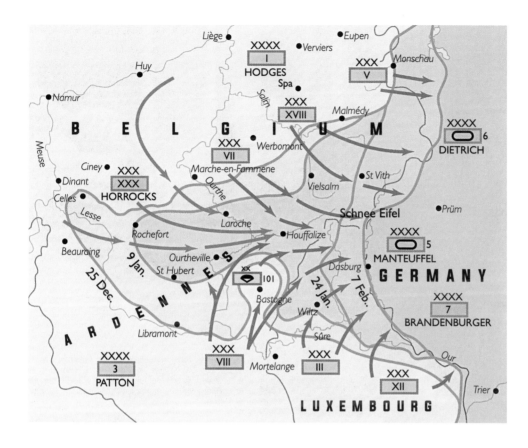

The Battle of the Bulge,
25 December 1944–7 February 1945

—————— front lines, with date

THE BASTOGNE POCKET

During the Battle of the Bulge, the advancing
German army failed to capture the small Belgian
town of Bastogne, held from 19 December by
the men of the US 101st Airborne Division
and elements of the Ninth and Tenth armored
divisions. The town was a vital road centre which
the German Panzer armies needed, and time
and effort had to be devoted to besieging it
which could have been diverted to speeding up
the advance. Low on ammunition and supplies,
but hopeful of relief from advancing US forces,
the commander, Brigadier General Anthony
McAuliffe, famously replied to German demands
to surrender on 22 December with the single
word "Nuts!". Despite desperate German efforts
to break the defending circle, Bastogne held
out until the counter-offensive arrived on
26 December to relieve it.

RIGHT An American force held out at Bastogne,
although surrounded and outnumbered.

Patton could swing his Third Army north to attack the south of what was now a large "bulge" (hence the name) in the American line; Montgomery took command of US forces in the north and co-ordinated Lieutenant General Hodges's US Seventh Corps and Lieutenant General Horrocks's Thirtieth Corps to blunt the German attack, and then began to assault the northern flank. Dietrich's SS troops were held at St Vith until 23 December, while Manteuffel's forces, despite their inability to take Bastogne, pushed on rapidly until they were within five kilometres (three miles) of the Meuse at Celles, where the Seventh Corps forced them to halt. At its greatest extent the Bulge was 65 kilometres (40 miles) wide and between 95 and 110 kilometres (60 and 70 miles) long. By this stage, the weather had cleared and thousands of British and American fighters and fighter-bombers were unleashed on the German units. Unable to capture additional oil stocks as planned, Manteuffel's tanks and vehicles also ran out of fuel. Both shoulders of the Bulge held, and by late December counter-offensives began to create the danger of another encirclement like the one at Falaise. Rundstedt asked Hitler for permission to withdraw which was refused, but by 8 January, with the neck of the Bulge rapidly closing, Hitler relented. Fighting a punishing rearguard campaign, German forces were back where they had started by 7 February.

The cost to both sides was high. Out of the half-million men committed, the German forces lost 100,000 casualties, around 850 tanks and almost all the 1,000 aircraft involved. This represented the end of serious German resistance in the west. US forces committed around 600,000 men to the contest and had casualties of 81,000, including 19,000 dead. British losses were 1,400, with 200 dead. The Battle of the Bulge was the costliest operation of the whole war in Western Europe.

LEFT A German medical corps officer holds an improvised white flag as he is approached by an American tank towards the end of the failed German offensive in January 1945.

CHRISTMAS NEWSLETTER

A newsletter of 24 December 1944 from the divisional headquarters of the US 101st Airborne Division gives details of the German demand for surrender at Bastogne, followed by the divisional commander's famous reply: "NUTS!"

HEADQUARTERS 101ST AIRBORNE DIVISION
Office of the Division Commander

24 December 1944

What's-Merry about all this, you ask? We're fighting - it's cold - we aren't home. All true but what has the proud Eagle Division accomplished with its worthy comrades of the 10th Armored Division, the 705th Tank Destroyer Battalion and all the rest? Just this: We have stopped cold everything that has been thrown at us from the North, East, South and West. We have identifications from four German Panzer Divisions, two German Infantry Division and one German Parachute Division. These units, spearheading the last desperate German lunge, were headed straight west for key points when the Eagle Division was hurriedly ordered to stem the advance. How effectively this was done will be written in history; not alone in our Division's glorious history but in World History. The Germans actually did surround us, their radios blared our doom. Their Commander demanded our surrender in the following impudent arrogance:

December 22nd 1944

"To the U. S. A. Commander of the encircled town of Bastogne.

The fortune of war is changing. This time the U. S. A. forces in and near Bastogne have been encircled by strong German armored units. More German armored units have crossed the river Our the near Ortheuville, have taken Marche and reached St. Hubert by passing through Homres-Sibret-Tillet. Libramont is in German hands.

There is only one possibility to save the encircled U. S. A. Troops from total annihilation: that is the honorable surrender of the encircled town. In order to think it over a term of two hours will be granted beginning with the presentation of this note.

If this proposal should be rejected one German Artillery Corps and six heavy A. A. Battalions are ready to annihilate the U. S. A. Troops in and near Bastogne. The order for firing will be given immediately after this two hour's term.

All the serious civilian losses caused by this Artillery fire would not correspond with the well known American humanity.

The German Commander"

The German Commander received the following reply:

22 December 1944

"To the German Commander:

<u>N U T S !</u>

The American Commander"

Allied Troops are counterattacking in force. We continue to hold Bastogne. By holding Bastogne we assure the success of the Allied Armies. We know that our Division Commander, General Taylor, will say: "Well Done!"
We are giving our country and our loved ones at home a worthy Christmas present and being privileged to take part in this gallant feat of arms are trully making for ourselves a Merry Christmas.

/s/ A. C. McAULIFFF
/t/　 . McAULIFFE,
　　　Commanding.

SOVIET ADVANCE ON GERMANY: VISTULA–ODER OPERATION

The operation that brought the Red Army from the River Vistula in eastern Poland across prewar Polish territory to the River Oder in eastern Germany was a victory almost as swift and comprehensive as the earlier German invasion of Poland in September 1939. In a little over two weeks, the German army in the east was finally broken and pushed back into Germany for the final defence of Berlin.

The German High Command knew that the Red Army, after its long pause in the autumn of 1944, would undertake a major operation aimed at the German capital. The head of German military intelligence in the east, General Gehlen, accurately predicted the date (mid-January) and the massive destructive effect that the Soviet army would have. Hitler ordered a series of defensive lines to be set up across Poland, with major cities designated as "fortress" strongpoints, to be defended to the death. Soviet planning took final shape in November with Marshal Zhukov, released from his work in Moscow as Stalin's deputy, appointed to command the 1st Belorussian Army Group at the centre of the whole operation. To his left was Marshal Konev's

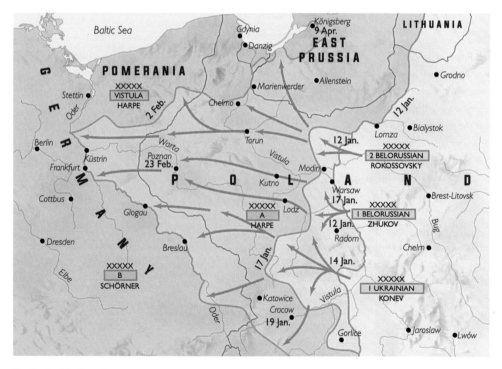

The Vistula–Oder Operation,
12 January–2 February 1945

——— front lines, with date

9 JANUARY 1945
US forces land on the main Philippine island of Luzon.

25 JANUARY 1945
The German Ardennes offensive ends with forces back at the line they started from.

27 JAUNARY 1945
Red Army liberates the extermination/concentration camp of Auschwitz.

30 JANUARY–3 FEBRUARY
Roosevelt and Churchill meet at Malta before the Yalta Conference.

9 FEBRUARY 1945
Colmar pocket in western Germany finally cleared by US Seventh Army.

13 FEBRUARY 1945
Soviet armies capture the Hungarian capital Budapest.

German rocket fire from the Baltic coast directed at the approaching Red Army, 8 March 1945. After the success of the Vistula-Oder operation Stalin ordered the Baltic coast to be cleared of German forces before the final assault on Berlin could take place.

1st Ukrainian Army Group, and to the north Rokossovsky's 2nd Belorussian Army Group. Konev was to drive to Silesia and to capture its rich industrial resources, if possible intact; Rokossovsky was to drive towards East Prussia and Pomerania; Zhukov's armies aimed directly towards Berlin.

By January 1945, the disparity between the strength of the two sides had become a chasm. Along the whole Eastern Front the Red Army could field six million men against two million Germans and 190,000 from their Axis partners. For the Vistula-Oder Operation there were 2.2 million Red Army troops, 33,500 guns and mortars, 7,000 tanks and self-propelled artillery and 5,000 aircraft. The German Army Group A (renamed Army Group Centre on 26 January) could field only 400,000 men, 270 aircraft and 1,136 tanks and self-propelled guns, while in East Prussia and Pomerania there were a further 580,000 troops, 700 tanks and 515 aircraft. The speed and completeness with which this force was defeated in January and February 1945 owed a good deal to the sheer weight of weaponry available to the Soviet side.

The operation unfolded in waves, like the "Bagration" campaign in Belorussia in summer 1944, designed to unhinge the German defences. Konev's 1st Ukrainian Army Group attacked on 12 January, and Zhukov's 1st Belorussian Army Group on 14 January. On the day in between, the

MARSHAL IVAN KONEV
(1897–1973)

Next to Marshal Zhukov, perhaps the best known of Soviet generals from the Second World War was Ivan Konev. The son of poor peasants from northern Russia, Konev worked as a lumberjack before being conscripted into the Russian army in 1916. He was still in training when Lenin's revolution took place in October 1917 and he became a keen and lifelong supporter of Communism. He became a military commissar during the Russian Civil War and stayed in the army after it was over. He was one of many young officers who were helped by the purges of 1937–38. By 1941, he was commander of the 19th Army in the Ukraine and was among the leading units to be hit first by the German invasion. Despite the disasters that overtook his forces, Konev survived Stalin's displeasure and was a key figure in the defence of Moscow, in charge of the Western Army Group. He was a major commander in the battles of 1942 and 1943 and led the 2nd Ukrainian Army Group for the drive across Ukraine to the frontiers of Eastern Europe. He was created a marshal in February 1944. After the war he became commander of Soviet land forces, and later commander-in-chief of Warsaw Pact forces, helping to repress the Hungarian revolution in 1956. He retired in 1963, and was buried in the Kremlin Wall on his death in 1973.

FIELD MARSHAL FERDINAND SCHÖRNER
(1892–1973)

Notorious as one of the most brutal of German army commanders, Schörner fought in a Bavarian regiment in the First World War in France, Italy and the east and was severely wounded three times. He remained in the army after 1919 and took part in suppressing the Hitler *Putsch* in Munich in November 1923. By the outbreak of war, he was a colonel in command of the 98th Regiment of Mountain Troops. In May 1940, he took over command of the 6th Mountain Division, which he led in France and the Balkans. From January 1942, he commanded the 19th Mountain Corps and was promoted to lieutenant general. He was noted for his National Socialist sympathies and tough leadership style (he liked the phrase "More fear of what is behind than what is in front!") and on 1 February 1944 was named chief of the newly created National Socialist Army Leadership Staff. He led army groups in the east in 1944, and in January 1945 took command of Army Group Centre in Poland. In April, he was made a field marshal. After the war he was sentenced to 25 years' hard labour in the Soviet Union, but released in 1955.

northern Soviet army groups began the operation to clear East Prussia, a move that brought the Red Army into German territory and with it a regime of atrocity and terror directed at the civilian population, including the mass rape of German women. Within two weeks, Konev had driven deep into Silesia and began a long siege of Breslau, which lasted from 13 February until 6 May, shortly before the German surrender. In the centre of the operation, Zhukov's armies finally seized Warsaw on 17 January from determined German defence of the ruined capital. Included among the attackers was the Polish 1st Army, recruited from among Poles sympathetic to communism. General Schörner was sent to take over Army Group A to try to steady the front line, but with little effect. Over the next two weeks, Zhukov pushed his forces forward, his faster motorized units pushing deep into the German rear. By 31 January, his first units reached the Oder near the fortified town of Küstrin, only 65 kilometres (40 miles) from Berlin, and by 2 February a small bridgehead had been forged across the Oder by troops who crossed the treacherously thin ice.

Slower progress was made in East Prussia and Pomerania, where the German army fiercely defended German soil. In front of the advancing Red Army flowed a stream of German refugees, terrified of Soviet vengeance. They arrived at the Baltic coast and a slow evacuation began, but for many German civilians the only way to escape was on foot through the narrow slice of territory that still divided Rokossovsky's forces from the sea. Everywhere small pockets of German resistance remained in the fortress zones. They were bypassed by the Red Army, to be picked off one by one when the campaign was over. The stage was now set for the final advance on the capital of Hitler's New Order.

Soviet T-34/85 tanks on the road towards Königsberg in late January/early February 1945. To save on vehicles and fuel, Soviet infantry assigned to armoured formations travelled on top of the tanks. The mixed-arm units introduced gradually from 1943 gave the Red Army the flexibility and fighting power enjoyed earlier by Germany's Panzer divisions.

19 FEBRUARY–26 MARCH 1945

IWO JIMA

As American forces closed in on the Japanese home islands in 1944, a choice had to be made between invading Formosa (Taiwan) or other islands closer to Japan. The Formosa plan was finally abandoned in October in favour of attacks on the Bonin and Ryukyu Islands. On 3 October 1944, Admiral Nimitz was instructed to choose an island for attack which could be used by fighter aircraft to support the bombers flying from the Marianas. He chose Iwo Jima, an eight-kilometre- (five-mile-) long volcanic island 1,060 kilometres (660 miles) south of Tokyo where Japanese aircraft were based for attacks on American air bases in the Marianas.

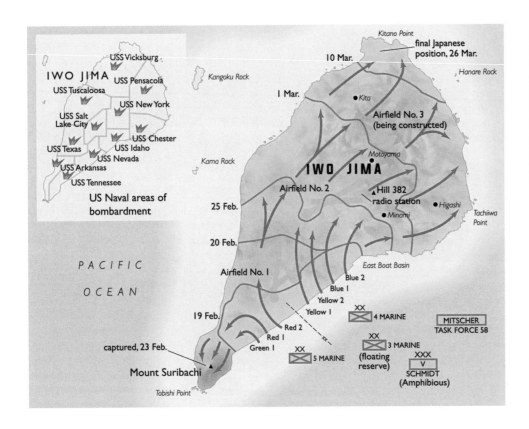

4 MARCH 1945
Allied forces capture Meiktila in Burma (Myanmar).

5 MARCH 1945
US armies reach the River Rhine in Germany and capture Cologne.

30 MARCH 1945
Red Army captures Danzig where the war began in 1939.

Iwo Jima,
19 February–26 March 1945

——— front lines, with date

The Japanese High Command guessed that the United States would try to find bases closer to the home islands. The local garrisons were strengthened and complex networks of tunnels and bunkers constructed. On Iwo Jima, Lieutenant General Tadamichi Kuribayashi commanded 22,000 troops dug in to well-prepared positions. The Japanese plan here, as elsewhere, was to allow the Americans to land and then to wear down their will to continue the fight in a brutal war of attrition. The 72 continuous days of aerial bombardment prior to the invasion of the island seem to have done little to dent the fighting power of the hidden defenders.

RIGHT Naval medical corps doctors and assistants at an emergency frontline dressing station. The poles have been stuck in the sand to support plasma bottles for blood transfusions. More than 17,000 marines were wounded, almost one-third of the attacking force.

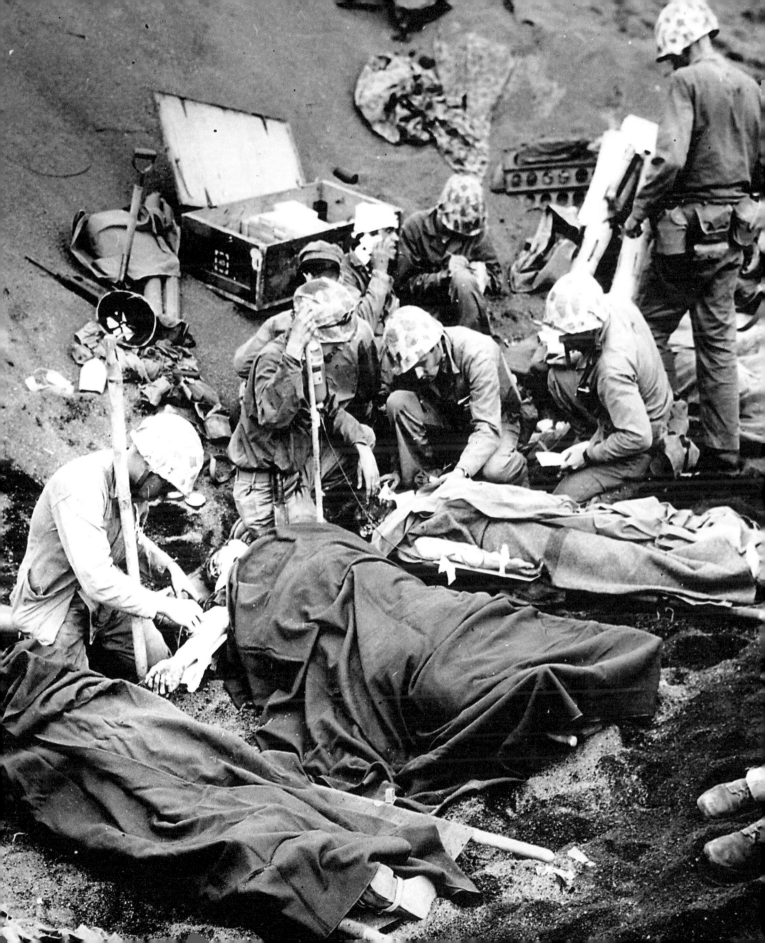

MOUNT SURIBACHI

One of the most famous images of the Second World War is the raising of the flag on top of Mount Suribachi, a small extinct volcano at the southern tip of Iwo Jima. The photograph was a staged replay of the first flag-raising by Company E of the 28th Marines on the morning of 23 February 1945, who seized the summit even though the mountain was still occupied by Japanese units. The first small flag was attached to a piece of waste pipe, but later that day a second patrol unit arrived at the peak with a larger flag and a war photographer, Joe Rosenthal. He photographed the men raising the second flag and created an iconic image.

The invasion force comprised the Fourth and Fifth Marine Divisions of Major General Harry Schmidt's Fifth Amphibious Corps, backed up by a reserve division, a total of 60,000 marines. There were 800 warships eventually committed to the battle. The invasion had to be postponed because of the slow progress in capturing the Philippines, but on 19 February, supported by the first naval "rolling barrage" of the Pacific War, the marines went ashore. The thick volcanic ash and steep shoreline made progress slow, and after 20 minutes the force was suddenly subjected to heavy flanking fire from hidden defences; some 519 marines were killed on the first day. Nevertheless, the first marines ashore succeeded in establishing a beachhead which soon housed almost 30,000 men. Most of Kuribayashi's force remained concealed in the defensive lines built further inland in deep bunkers and pillboxes carved into the soft volcanic rock. The first airstrip was captured on 20 February and Mount Suribachi four days later. By 27 February, the other completed airstrips had been captured, but it took another month before the island was declared secure.

Japanese resistance so close to the home islands increased in intensity and the marines took exceptionally heavy casualties. On Hill 382, nicknamed the "Meat Grinder", the marines had to fight for every yard against defenders who fought until they were killed. Each defensive position in the gorges and caves of the rocky island had to be captured using flamethrowers and explosives to kill or flush out the defenders. Even when forced into the open, many Japanese soldiers hurled themselves at the attackers rather than surrender. The sheer weight of American firepower from sea, air and land drove the Japanese defenders back to the north of the island where they made their last stand in "Bloody Gorge" at Kitano Point which took ten days to clear and ended with a final suicidal *banzai* charge. Even though the island was declared secure on 26 March,

GENERAL HARRY SCHMIDT
(1886–1968)

Harry Schmidt was Marine commander of the Fifth Amphibious Corps in the battle for Iwo Jima. He joined the Marine Corps in 1909 and had his first posting to Guam in the Pacific in 1911. After a long career on and off water he was head of the Paymaster Department of the Marine Corps when war broke out in 1941. In January 1942, he became assistant to the Marine Corps commander and in August 1943 commanding general of the Fourth Marine Division. His forces took part in the capture of Saipan and Tinian, by which time he was commander of the Fifth Amphibious Corps. His corps distinguished itself in the capture of Iwo Jima and went on to become part of the occupying force in Japan after the war was over. In February 1946, he took over the Marine Training Command and retired in 1948, when he was promoted to four-star general.

a further 2,409 Japanese soldiers were killed in the period up to June as defenders fought almost literally to the last man. The Japanese suffered a total of 23,300 killed, with nearly no prisoners taken. Marine losses totalled 5,931 dead and 17,372 wounded over one-third of the original force committed.

Fighter aircraft began to operate from Iwo Jima even before it was secured and the first B-29 "Superfortress" bomber landed on the island on 4 March, the first of 2,251 which made emergency landings on the island on the way to or from the Japanese home islands. At a high cost in lives, the air route to Japan was finally secured and the last stages of the heavy bombing of Japan's cities could be undertaken.

A small group of Japanese prisoners out of 216 taken alive on Iwo Jima from the garrison of 23,000. These prisoners were taken during mopping-up operations in the weeks following the defeat of organized resistance. They have been issued with cigarettes by their American captors.

COMBAT REPORT FROM IWO JIMA

A combat report from the US 28th Marine Regiment filed during the taking of Iwo Jima. Dated 20–21 February 1945, two days after the initial landings, this report was filed as marines approached Mount Suribachi in the south of the island, which was captured three days later.

Left page (100):

Journal

Organization _____

From ___13 MAR 45 D+22___

To ___

Place _____   DECLASSIFIED

100

TIME In	Out	SERIAL NO.	TIME DATED	INCIDENTS, MESSAGES, ORDERS, ETC.	ACTION TAKEN
0700		1	PH	2d 328 — slight infiltration, otherwise quiet.	—
0730		2	PH	Fr Lt 328 — All quiet —	—
0735		3	PH	Fr Lt 328 — G Co, 30 or 4 Nips attempted infiltration — H Co. one light arty round in CP — No known casualties I Co — Killed 5 Nips last nite — Have blown 30 cave entrances (12 Sunday, 18 Monday —	D 2
	0740	4	PH	To D² — Report.	—
0744	0845	5	MC	To Lt 128 228, 328, O — Overlay front lines (Periodic Report sent last nite)	—
0944	0955	6	R	Fr Lt 328 — G Co Report PB in 235 E — They obs. enemy activity around it this morning — & tracks are now firing on it	R 3
0955		7	R	Fr Div — Air Obs Reports at 235 AC — mouth of cave just inside it bends are 2 concrete pillboxes apparently unamaged.	R 3
0955		8	R	Fr Div — Air Obs Reports at 208 O at Ch on west side : 224 D ½ on high ground . 234 I just across from one in 0 Blockhouses located at each above position apparently unamaged.	R 3
0954		9	R	Fr Div — Air Obs Reports — 234 J² concrete structure east side of road apparently unamaged.	R 3

Right page (101):

Journal

Organization _____

From ___13 MAR 45 D+22___

To ___

Place _____   DECLASSIFIED

101

TIME In	Out	SERIAL NO.	TIME DATED	INCIDENTS, MESSAGES, ORDERS, ETC.	ACTION TAKEN
1015		10	1015 R	Fr Div Air Obs Report — 251 P½ Blockhouse taken under arty fire several days ago — Evidently put back in shape by enemy (328 Z)	R 3
1010		11	PH	Fr Lt 328 — Jap 37 mm gun in good position in Hari Co CP at 234 T ½	D 2
1035		12	PH	Fr Lt 328 — G Co on left received machine gun coverage from left flank of 328 Z of A — No known casualties. As viewed from O P	—
1045		13	Runner	Fr D² — Periodic Report Plus Overlay + POW & Document Trans.	
	1105	14	MC	To Lt 128, 228, 328 — Periodic Reports from D² as of 1800 last nite	
1110		15	MC	Fr Div — Air Obs. — 251 G — Japs observed standing in and around cave entrance which faces North	
1110		16	R	Fr Div — Air Obs — 251 P½ and 251 V½ 2 Blockhouse evidently operative — Cave entrance P have been blocked here for the most part — otherwise saw no signs of activity — Results of air strike requested yesterday	R 3
1145		17	PH	Fr Lt 328 — Progress only 20 or 30 feet — Enemy fire not so heavy — Tanks attempting to move down road.	R 3

_____Journal
Organization_____
From _13 MAR 45 - D+22_
To_____
Place_____   DECLASSIFIED

TIME In	Out	SERIAL NO.	TIME DATED	INCIDENTS, MESSAGES, ORDERS, ETC.	ACTION TAKEN
1147		18	R.	FR Div - Air OBS Reports - 234 J²⁵ Blockhouse Located - Gun from there can cover almost anything in CT 28 Area	R3
1200		19	R	FR Div - Air OBS reports 250 5ᵀᴱ gun was moved out of cave at waters edge just north of finger of Rocks which sticks out into water, this gun was previously being moved out to fire at destroyer and pulled back when Air obs. flew over.	R3
1220		20	R	FR Div - In 250 Yᴱ mortar fire seeming to be coming out from small Ridge firing into central area of our lines.	R3
1246		21	R	FR Lt 328 - 1 Round of friendly Arty Low landed 150 yds in front of our CP Arty landed in approx same area as those of last nite	R3
1250		22	R	FR Div - Sockeye reports in 234 Dᴺ⁻ just N. of unimproved road is what appears to be a blockhouse. This may have been previously reported by another sockeye	R3
1255		23	R	FR Lt 328 - Duplex (328) reports that a friendly napalm tank was burning and blew up in TA 234 Oᴺᴱ or 234 Kᴱᴺ	R3
1325		24	Ph	FR Lt 128 - Camouflage exposed by our fire shows G.H. at 23 4J⁵ Explosion Lower front unexplained "Demolition"	

_____Journal
Organization_____
From _13 MARCH 45 - D+22_
To_____
Place_____   DECLASSIFIED

TIME In	Out	SERIAL NO.	TIME DATED	INCIDENTS, MESSAGES, ORDERS, ETC.	ACTION TAKEN
1340		25	(TO) Ph	FR Lt 328 - Rocket effective as dug in snipers. Stim Co expects to be able to move out. G Co still pinned down - snipers tanks	R3
1430		26	Ph	FR Lt LLOYD - KAMA and KANGOKU Rock - Evidence of nips on KANGOKU Rock 1000. Corps Rcn Bn landed after heavy preparation 226 - 127 - 327 in that order on our flanks	—
1445		27	PH	FR Lt 228 - F Co attempting to move. Gained around 50 yds. Rifle and MG, occasional mortar burst around.	R3
1450		28	PH	FR Lt 328 - G Co preparing to move out - Understand E Co of 226 on right is moving out	—
1455		29	PH	FR R2 CT 27 - Our lines moving out Don't know how far - opposition Blackened semetatt	—
1458		30	R	FR Div - Air OBS reports at 256 X⁴ EAST of Road about 25 yds Are 2 caves, 1 large and 1 sm opening to the N.	R3
1515		31	R	FR Div - Air OBS Reports MG Fire from 225 7ᴺᴱ apparently directed to CT 28 Left Flank —	R3
1600		32	R Int	Enemy Casualties to date. CT 28 - 4783 CT 26 - 2258 CT 27 - 1847	7

_____Journal

Organization_____

From 13 MAR 45 D+22

To_____

Place_____ DECLASSIFIED

TIME In	Out	SERIAL NO.	TIME DATED	INCIDENTS, MESSAGES, ORDERS, ETC.	ACTION TAKEN
1640		33	MC Nws	Fr D² Weather - Cloudy - NE to E Surface winds 12-18 Knots - Visibility, six miles	—
1742	1645	34	Runner	To D² - Periodic Report and Overlay	—
"	1715	35	MC	To Lt 126, 208, 328 - Periodic Report and Overlay -	—
1730		36	R 1645	Fr Lt 328 - OP Reports that enemy mortar fire landed 50 yards to left of OP - No way to know where it came from - CP at 234 SE	—
1635		37	PH	Fr Lt 328 - Moving slowly - I Co meeting heavy resistance. Flame throwing tank assisting greatly (Flame throwing Tanks flushed 6 snipers out of GG Co 2 of A and killed them - 100 yard gap between Geo G and Easy G 227 being filled up.	—
1650		38	PH	Fr 1 Lt - Nips pulling back to 250 T - A Co receiving 90 mm mortar fire - Probably from Nips taken hill in 250 T".	—
1900		39	INT. R	CT17 - Front Lines - 235 Reg from Lt. MSW corner to SE corner, NW corner to SE corner, SW corner to SE corner to 236 P⁶.	—

_____Journal

Organization_____

From 13 Mar 45 - D+22

To_____

Place_____ DECLASSIFIED

TIME In	Out	SERIAL NO.	TIME DATED	INCIDENTS, MESSAGES, ORDERS, ETC.	ACTION TAKEN
1915		40	R-	Fr Lt 328 - Friendly air burst about 50 yards to right of CP burst at 1915	R3
2010		41	MC	Fr CG Div - Confidential - Comply King Pin R and LW for directives - Report Enemy dead counted in to time by your organization	—
				14 MAR 45 D+23	
0730		1	PH	Fr Lt 328 - Quiet - 26 enemy dead - 4 caves blown, fuel dump burning.	—
0735		2	PH	Fr Lt 328 - Minor grenade battles, otherwise quiet	—
0740		3	PH	Fr Lt 128 - All quiet	—
	0745	4	PH	To Div - Morning Report, also advised 3150 enemy dead seen.	—
0805		5	PH	Fr Lt 328 - Moving up	—
0805		6	R 0805	Fr Div - Front lines - 250 WS 234 C⁶², Lt N³, 205 K⁴¹², Lt M⁴², R¹⁶, X¹⁶, Y⁴⁶, 236 U⁶, V⁶, W⁶	—
0855		7	R Int.	Fr Div to CT 27 - Air Obs. reports in TA 235 MᵃR cave observed in bluff - several Japs running into it	—
0900		8	—	Lt. O'Donnell, Lt Klebr, Capt Donald, and units of Hqrs Co. left CP for Front Line Duty at 1700-3-13-45	—

COMBAT REPORT FROM IWO JIMA

The second combat report from Iwo Jima was filed near the end of the battle on 13 March 1945, as surviving Japanese soldiers and snipers were flushed out of caves and bunkers in the north of the island.

R-2 Verodic Report

From: 1800, Feb. 20, 1945
To: 1600, Feb. 21, 1945

No. 2

Maps: 1:10,000. Iwo Jima Battle Map.

1. Enemy Situation at End of Period.
   a. Enemy front lines (or nearest elements.)
      See overlay
   B. Defensive Organizations.
      See overlay.
   c. Units in contact.
      At 131 I, J, & 132 F are unitopposed by 1st Co. 312 Inf. Various naval guard troops and elements of 132 & 125 AA are also in our area. Haha unit also identified. On 132 L & M we face 3rd Co. 312th.
   D. Artillery.
      Less intense than yesterday however between 2100 & 0300 last night intense fire received from the North, mortar fire also very heavy around CT 28 CP.
   E. Reserves & other forces capable of intervention. unknown.
   F. Supply and evacuation establishments. none identified.

      — 1 —

2. Enemy operations During Period.
   a. Period Summary.
      At 2100 Japs counter-attacked from 132 I - attack repulsed. Later at 2300 five to Japs seen milling around on beach. At 132 M and were fired on by NGF. At 0830 our attack bogged at base of SURIBACHI. Area to knocked out in the morning. Even still resistance from base of mountain and from caves.
   c. operation of component elements.
      (1) No antiaircraft artillery.
      (2) no antitank units definitely identified
      (3) no armored forces.
      (4) Artillery
          Intermittent throughout the day. 70 & 75 mm guns knocked out at base of mountain. number unknown.
      (5) no aviation, combat.
      (6) No Aviation, observation, including balloon
      (7) no cavalry
      (8) no Chemical warfare.
      (9) Engineers
          Encountering a lot of mines in area. Booby traps found but not hooked up.
          — 2 —

   (10) Infantry.
        Japs infantry still fighting fanatically from well prepared pillboxes and block-houses. Have to blow them out, none surrendered.

3. Miscellaneous.
   a. Estimated enemy casualties, including prisoners. no prisoners as yet. Trying to get them out of caves but its hard. To date have counted 207 dead in area. Lots in pillboxes but havent been able to get count yet.
   B. Morale. Captured document stated he expected to die & that others from home would replace them. They were to do their utmost.
   C. Supply and Equipment.
      Question. Enough ammo though.
   D. Terrain not under our control. still good for Japs.
   E. Enemys probable knowledge of our situation. Good cant do much.
   F. Weather & Visibility.
      Poor but can see fair from our OP to Hill.

4 Enemy Capabilities.
   (1) Counter attack along beach Harasses + infiltrate our present position. (2) Little hope for him now its just a matter of time (3) Air cross interdicting also consideration but dont know enough about it at present

      — 3 —   R-2

9–10 MARCH 1945

THE FIREBOMBING OF TOKYO

The bombing of Japan, like the bombing of Germany in Europe, began slowly and with mixed results. Because of the long distances involved, the bombers then in use in the European theatre were unable to reach mainland Japan from existing bases. Only when the first B-29 "Superfortress" bombers became available from the summer of 1944 – the first 130 arrived in India in May – was it possible to mount long-distance attacks against targets in the Japanese Empire in Manchuria, Korea or Thailand; the Japanese home islands were still difficult to reach for aircraft at the limit of their range. The capture of the Marianas was essential for the planned campaign of precision bombing against Japanese steel production and the aviation industry.

The first major B-29 raid was against the Thai capital of Bangkok on 5 June 1944. From then until early 1945, the Twentieth Air Force operated from bases in India and China against distant targets with very limited success. Operation "Matterhorn", as it was codenamed, achieved little and when the Japanese army overran the Chinese airfields the operation was wound up. Instead General Arnold, the USAAF chief-of-staff, decided to deploy the B-29s from the Marianas using Twenty-first Bomber Command under General Haywood Hansell, one of the planners of the air war in Europe. The first B-29 landed in October 1944 on Saipan, but a combination of slow delivery of aircraft, regular harassing attacks by Japanese aircraft, now using ramming techniques against enemy bombers, and the exceptionally long flights to mainland Japan in generally poor weather once again led to very limited achievements. In the first three months of operations, only 1,146 tons of bombs were dropped on a range of precision targets. The first raid on Tokyo took place on 24 November 1944 but the effects were slight.

The disappointing nature of the bombing campaign led Arnold to sack Hansell and replace him with the more aggressive Major General

13–15 FEBRUARY 1945
Firebombing of the German city of Dresden.

25 FEBRUARY 1945
Firebombing raid on Tokyo destroys one square mile of the city.

8 MARCH 1945
First efforts made by German emissaries to bring about an armistice in northern Italy.

14–15 MARCH
B-29 bombers attack the city of Osaka, inflicting further heavy casualties.

LEFT A Boeing B-29 heavy bomber at a base in China as it prepares to take off for a bombing mission over Japan. Most B-29 attacks were later made from the Mariana Islands in the central Pacific but from June 1944 attacks were made from China until the main airfields were overrun by Japanese armies later in the year. The B-29 had a range of 9,000 kilometres (5,600 miles) but could carry 5,500 kilograms (12,000 pounds) of bombs only 2,000 kilometres (1,600 miles).

BELOW Japanese children being evacuated from Ueno station in Tokyo. Around 8 million Japanese moved from threatened urban areas to the overcrowded countryside, placing a severe strain on an already overstretched rationing system.

GENERAL HENRY "HAP" ARNOLD
(1886–1950)

As chief-of-staff of the United States Army Air Force throughout the Second World War, Arnold played a central role in the American war effort. He became an army airman in the First World War, and by 1918 was assistant commander-in-chief of the Air Service, though he arrived too late in Europe to see combat. In September 1938, he was chosen to head the Army Air Corps with the rank of major general, and when the corps was turned into the Army Air Forces in June 1941, Arnold became its chief. He sat on both the American Joint Chiefs-of-Staff Committee and the Anglo-American Combined Chiefs Committee. In March 1942, his official title became Commanding General of the US Army Air Forces. He was an energetic, hardworking and sociable commander ("Hap" was short for "Happy"), with a clear understanding of technical development and high managerial skills. He suffered from poor health towards the end of the war, when he became the air force's first five-star general.

Curtis LeMay, who arrived on Saipan in January 1945. After more weeks of unspectacular high-altitude precision attacks, LeMay was arguing with senior commanders for a radical change in tactics. He advocated using the newly available and highly effective M-69 firebomb in large quantities in low-level night-time attacks on Japan's urban areas. The subsequent fires would destroy local industry, demoralize the population and perhaps accelerate surrender. Uncertain whether Arnold would approve "area bombing", LeMay planned an experiment against Tokyo on the night of 9–10 March. A total of 334 B-29s were launched from three island bases carrying over 1,600 tons of incendiaries and 279 reached their destination.

The aircraft arrived over Tokyo in the early hours of 10 March, flying at between 1,200 and 2,800 metres (4,000 and 9,200 feet), where they met little resistance from the air defences. Pathfinders marked the area to be bombed with napalm, and the bombers released their loads indiscriminately within the designated zone. The attack quickly provoked a firestorm which burned out 41 square kilometres (16 square miles) of the city and killed an estimated 100,000 people in a single night, the highest death toll of any single air attack. One million people were rendered homeless and a quarter of all residential buildings

RIGHT An aerial view of central Tokyo following the firebombing of the city on the night of 9–10 March 1945. Only the concrete structures remain among the ruins of a highly flammable city where more than 100,000 lost their lives. The heat became so intense that people fleeing into the Sumida River (top) were boiled alive in the water.

GENERAL CURTIS LEMAY
(1906–90)

Curtis E. LeMay masterminded the bombing of Japan and went on to play a central role in creating the US Strategic Air Command after the war. He joined the US Army Air Corps (later the Army Air Forces) in 1928 and had risen by October 1942 to the rank of colonel in charge of a bomber group of the Eighth Air Force based in England. A commander who flew with his men to experience combat, and a thoughtful tactician, LeMay was rapidly promoted. He was already a major general, the youngest in the army, when in August 1944 he took over command of Twentieth Bomber Command based in India for attacks from Chinese bases on Japanese targets in Manchuria and the home islands. He moved in January 1945 to take command of the Twenty-first Bomber Command on the Marianas and from here organized the bombing of Japan's cities. In July, he took command of Twentieth US Army Air Forces (which included Twenty-first and Twentieth Bomber Command) and later the same month became chief-of-staff to the newly formed Strategic Air Forces in the Pacific. After the war he became commander of the Strategic Air Command from 1949 to 1957, and in 1961 chief-of-staff of the US Air Force.

were destroyed. Over the next six months, LeMay's force destroyed 58 Japanese cities and inflicted an estimated 500,000 deaths. The new tactics of fire bombing at low altitude proved grimly effective. An attack, for example, on the northern Honshu town of Aomori on the night of 28–29 July destroyed 88 per cent of the built-up area. By this time there were 3,700 B-29s available, more than the Marianas could accommodate. There remains much argument over whether the urban attacks were responsible for reducing Japanese war production, since the loss of the merchant marine and attacks on communications played an important part in this, but there is no doubt that the bomb attacks quickly demoralized the home population and accelerated the efforts of those Japanese leaders who could see the war was lost to try to find some acceptable formula for surrender.

LEFT US carrier-based aircraft on a bombing raid against Tokyo on 2 March 1945. Aircraft from Task Force 58 and Task Force 38 bombarded Japanese cities and defences from March to August 1945 against light Japanese resistance. Aircraft also engaged in the heavy mining of Japanese coastal waters, bringing trade almost to a halt.

7 MARCH–25 APRIL 1945

THE WESTERN ADVANCE INTO GERMANY: FROM THE RHINE TO THE ELBE

At the end of 1944, the Western Allies were poised to begin the assault on Germany when the Battle of the Bulge interrupted their preparations. The effect was not entirely negative, for the final fling of German forces in the west removed the last major reserves of tanks and aircraft and left the three German army groups – General Student's Group H in the north in the Netherlands, Group B under Field Marshal Model in the Ruhr and Group G under General Blaskowitz in the south – well under strength and devoid of serious air support.

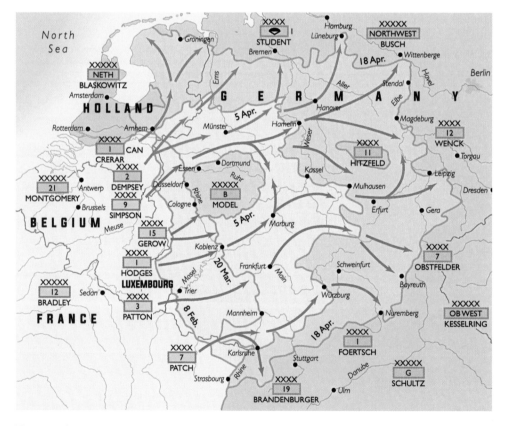

The western advance into Germany,
7 February–18 April 1945

——— front lines, with date

19 MARCH 1945
Hitler issues his "scorched earth" directive ordering Germans to destroy everything in the path of the advancing Allied armies.

27 MARCH 1945
Argentina finally declares war on Germany and Japan.

12 APRIL 1945
Death of President Roosevelt. Vice President Truman takes his place.

13 APRIL 1945
Vienna captured by the 2nd and 3rd Ukrainian army groups.

Eisenhower favoured an approach on a broad front, as the Red Army was doing in the east. By 3 January, he had 73 divisions, 20 of them armoured and the rest well-equipped, supported by overwhelming strength in the air, both tactical and strategic. The campaign to bring the war to an end involved three stages: clearing the territory on the west bank of the Rhine, effecting a series of Rhine crossings to establish solid bridgeheads on the eastern bank, and finally a general breakout to bring Western armies to the River Elbe and into Austria and Czechoslovakia, where they would meet up with the Soviet armed forces. Although Montgomery would have preferred a breakthrough on a narrower front and rapid deployment towards Berlin, Eisenhower accepted the decision agreed at Yalta that Berlin would be in the Soviet zone of operations.

The first series of operations was launched on 8 February 1945 when Montgomery's Twenty-first Army Group, under the codename "Veritable", began an attack to clear the area between the River Meuse and the Rhine. The British 2nd Army and Canadian 1st Army encountered fierce resistance from the German 1st Paratroop Army in the Reichswald forest and not until 21 February was the northern area west of the Rhine cleared. The US Ninth Army, mounting Operation "Grenade", was held up by flooding and could only begin on 23 February, but weak German resistance brought them to the bank of the Rhine near Düsseldorf on 1 March. Further south, Bradley's Twelfth Army Group, in Operation "Lumberjack", cut rapidly through the defences of the Westwall, the main frontier fortifications, to reach the river by 7 March, while Operation "Undertone", led by Lieutenant

GENERAL JACOB DEVERS
(1887–1979)

A career field artillery officer, who joined the US Army in 1909, Devers was an outstanding administrator. As the army's youngest major general, he oversaw the expansion of the American Armored Force from just two divisions to 16 by 1943. In May 1943, he was appointed overall commander of US Army forces in Europe where he helped to organize and train units for the D-Day landings. At the end of the year, he became deputy supreme commander in the Mediterranean and in September 1944 he was posted to active command of Sixth Army Group, which was moving through southern France towards Alsace. He led the army group across the Rhine and accepted the surrender of German forces in Austria on 6 May 1945; he was shortly thereafter promoted to full general. He retired from the army in 1949.

General Jacob Devers's Sixth Army Group, pushed forward into the Saarland to reach Mannheim on the southern Rhine.

It was during the "Lumberjack" operation that the US Ninth Armored Division surprised German troops trying to demolish the Hindenburg railway bridge over the river at Remagen. They captured the bridge intact

BELOW A landing craft helps to tow a bridge section in the Reichswald sector of the River Rhine, 25 March 1945. A Taylorcraft Auster spotter aircraft flies above, while the engineers construct a crossing for British Commonwealth armies.

OPPOSITE British troops of the Gordon Highlanders fighting in the Reichswald forest in northwest Germany, 9 February 1945. Fighting here was fierce against five defensive lines and in heavy mud. The forest was finally cleared by 9 March.

RIGHT Soviet and US servicemen fraternize on the banks of the Elbe river at Torgau on 25 April 1945, where elements of the US First Army and the Soviet 1st Ukrainian Army Group joined forces. First contact had been made a few hours earlier at the village of Stehla, but the heavily photographed gathering at Torgau has become popularly accepted as the initial meeting.

on 7 March and established a small bridgehead on the far side. Despite efforts to destroy the bridge with V-2 rockets, it survived until 17 March, when it finally collapsed. Eisenhower insisted on maintaining a broad front nevertheless, and Montgomery planned a massive assault across the river between Rees and Duisburg. German forces had been reduced to a mere 26 divisions, by contrast with more than 200 facing the Red Army in the east. To cope with the expected assault, Hitler replaced the faithful von Rundstedt with Field Marshal Kesselring, the defender of Italy. There were simply too few soldiers and too little equipment to hold up the assault for long. When the Rhine was crossed in force on 24 March in the north a broad bridgehead was easily secured. Ever mindful of the opportunity to get the better of the British, General Patton made his crossing further south at Oppenheim two days before, on the night of 22–23 March.

Unequal though the contest was, it would be wrong to see it as a straightforward campaign. German forces often fought with fanatical determination and great tactical skill and high casualties were exacted in the last month of the conflict, but the final outcome was not in doubt. The Ruhr pocket was split into two with the Germans in one part surrendering on 16 April and the other on 18 April. Model killed himself on 21 April and an estimated 350,000 men surrendered in total. Meanwhile, Montgomery's Twenty-first Army Group reached the ruins of Lübeck on the Baltic coast. Further south, resistance crumbled. The US Ninth Army reached Magdeburg on the Elbe river on 12 April, while forward units of Lieutenant General Hodges's US First Army reached the Elbe on 25 April near the town of Torgau, where they experienced a historic meeting with

GENERAL JOHANNES BLASKOWITZ
(1883–1948)

The son of a Prussian priest, Johannes Blaskowitz joined the army as a cadet at the age of 10, and was a lieutenant by the time he was 19. He was a company commander and staff officer on four different fronts during the First World War, stayed in the postwar army and was a major general by 1932. He was commander of Army Group 3 in Dresden from 1938 and in this capacity his forces helped occupy Austria and the Sudetenland in 1938, and Czechoslovakia in March 1939. He commanded the 8th Army in Poland and took the surrender of Warsaw. He was afterwards commander of the German army of occupation, during which time he protested regularly about the atrocities being perpetrated against Poles and Jews. He was removed by Hitler in May 1940 and posted as commander of the German 1st Army of occupation in France in October. In 1944, he took over Army Group G in southern France and successfully withdrew his forces northwards following Operation "Dragoon". In January 1945, he commanded Army Group H in the Netherlands, finally surrendering to the British on 5 May 1945. He was imprisoned after the war and committed suicide at Nuremberg in February 1948.

units of Konev's 1st Ukrainian Army Group. The US Sixth Army Group, which included the French 1st Army under General de Lattre de Tassigny, cleared southern Germany and moved into Austria. It was now only a matter of time before Germany was utterly defeated.

26 MARCH–30 JUNE 1945

OKINAWA

While the final battles were waged for Iwo Jima, a huge task force was made ready to invade Okinawa, largest of the Ryukyu Islands, on the edge of the Japanese home islands. The battle was the largest of the Pacific War and the costliest for the American and Japanese forces involved. Okinawa was chosen as a potential base for heavy air attacks on Japan, but it could also be used as a staging post for the eventual invasion of the main islands.

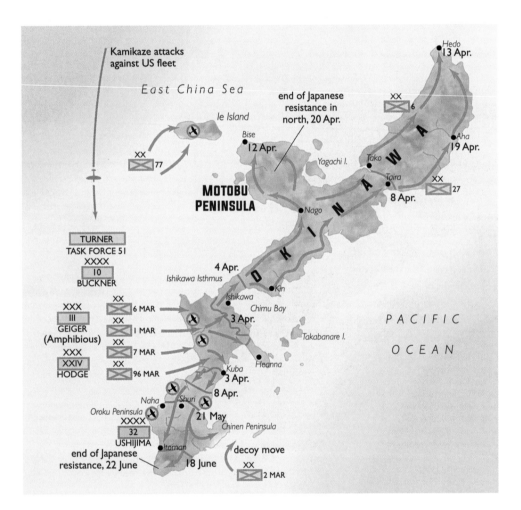

Okinawa, 1 April–30 June 1945

front lines, with date

24 APRIL 1945
Allied forces cross the Po river in northern Italy in the course of Operation "Grapeshot".

2 MAY 1945
German armies in Italy surrender.

3 MAY 1945
Allied forces capture Rangoon in Burma (Myanmar).

4 MAY 1945
German forces in northern Europe surrender to Montgomery's Twenty-first Army Group.

7 MAY 1945
General Jodl signs unconditional surrender of Germany at Rheims, France.

26 JUNE 1945
The United Nations Charter is signed in San Francisco by 50 states.

The preparations matched the scale of the "Overlord" landings in France the previous year. Under the overall command of Rear Admiral Raymond Spruance, Operation "Iceberg" eventually involved half-a-million men and 1,213 naval vessels. Lieutenant General Simon Buckner's recently activated US Tenth Army, made up of two marine and four regular army divisions, was given the task of clearing the island, but this time it was defended by approximately 100,000 Japanese troops, including 20,000 Okinawan militia, a much larger concentration than on

Iwo Jima or Saipan. The invasion was supported by Vice Admiral Marc Mitscher's Task Force 58, which began a heavy naval bombardment of the island on 23 March.

The Japanese commander, General Mitsuru Ushijima, decided against the instructions of the High Command to adopt the same tactics used on Iwo Jima, despite their evident failure. Most of the long, thin island was difficult to defend except for the limestone outcrops at the south end. Ushijima concentrated most of his forces in the hilly region of the south with a defensive line across the island from its chief town, Naha. Other forces were based on the Motobu Peninsula further up the west coast. The Japanese hoped to benefit from the decision, taken some months before, to use aircraft on kamikaze missions, employing the aircraft itself as a weapon to sink American shipping.

The campaign began with the seizure of the outlying Kerama and Keise islands between 23 and 29 March. The main attack came on the morning of 1 April on the west coast of Okinawa. The invasion force faced little opposition and moved inland to seize the airfields. By the following day, the island was split in two as US forces reached the east coast. The marine units moved northwards against weak resistance, reaching the north of the island by 15 April. Only on the Mobotu Peninsula was there heavy fighting, but the Marine Sixth Division secured it by 20 April.

The four army divisions faced a much more formidable obstacle when they reached the southern defensive line on 9 April. The terrain favoured the defenders and the American assault stalled. On 4 May, in torrential rains that turned the ground to mud, the Japanese launched a powerful

KAMIKAZE

In October 1944, the Japanese navy authorized the formation of a force of suicide pilots who would crash their aircraft deliberately into enemy ships in an effort to sink or disable them. The term chosen, *kamikaze* (divine wind), was a reference back to a medieval Mongol-Japanese war in which the Mongol fleet was dispersed by a fierce gale and Japan saved from invasion. The first official suicide attack was made on 25 October 1944 against the US escort carrier *St Lo*. Large numbers were used in the Battle of Leyte Gulf and the peak of suicide attacks came during the invasion of Okinawa in April 1945. The aircraft were fighters or trainer aircraft, loaded with bombs; the pilots were volunteers initially, then supplemented by conscripts. They flew a total of 2,314 sorties and hit 322 Allied ships, sinking 34. The effect of the campaign was to destroy much of what was left of the Japanese air force for a very limited tactical gain.

LEFT The carrier USS *Bunker Hill* on fire after being hit by two Japanese suicide planes off Okinawa on 11 May 1945. The Japanese aircraft crashed onto the carrier's aircraft which were preparing to take off for an attack on Okinawa.

counter-attack which produced a prolonged hand-to-hand battle with high casualties on both sides.

From 6 April, the invasion fleet was also subject to repeated kamikaze attacks launched by the commander of the Japanese 1st Mobile Fleet under the codename "Ten-Go". From then until 22 June, the fleet was subjected to 1,900 suicide attacks which caused high casualties among the crews, sank 36 naval vessels and damaged a further 368. The Japanese navy also launched a suicide mission when the giant battleship *Yamato*, together with a single cruiser and eight destroyers, set out to attack the US fleet. The ship was sighted on 7 April in the East China Sea and sunk in an attack by 380 carrier aircraft, a dramatic end to what had been in 1941 one of the most powerful navies in the world.

RIGHT Japanese open-faced flying helmet.

OPPOSITE US marines laden with equipment clamber down ladders into waiting landing craft on 10 April 1945 during the early stages of the three-month campaign on Okinawa. Over 170,000 US servicemen saw action in the capture of the island.

LIEUTENANT GENERAL SIMON BOLIVAR BUCKNER
(1886–1945)

Lieutenant General Simon Buckner was the highest-ranking US officer to be killed by enemy fire during the Second World War. The son of a Confederate general of the same name, Buckner joined the army in 1908, serving in the Philippines during the First World War. He was a tough trainer of men and was commandant of cadets at West Point in the early 1930s. He was sent to command the defence of Alaska in 1941 and was then promoted to brigadier general. In 1943, he seized back the two Aleutian islands captured by the Japanese in 1942. In July 1944 he organized the US Tenth Army for the conquest of Taiwan, but their destination was then changed to Okinawa and it was here, on 18 June 1945, towards the end of the campaign, that he was hit by shells from a Japanese battery and killed instantly.

Not until 21 May did the Japanese line begin to break. Naha was captured on 27 May and Ushijima retreated with his remaining forces to the Oroku Peninsula, where a final ferocious encounter brought an end to Japanese resistance on 22 June. Buckner was killed on 18 June; Ushijima killed himself four days later. These were two of a high toll of casualties. Only 7,400, mainly Okinawan militia, survived from the 100,000 strong Japanese garrison, while total American deaths amounted to 12,281 with 36,631 wounded. The very high cost of securing a tiny island made the invasion of the home islands seem an increasingly hazardous and costly undertaking and played a part in the decision, taken a month later, to drop the atomic bomb.

OPPOSITE An officer of the US Tenth Army shares his rations with two Okinawan children found hiding in an abandoned tomb on the island. Thousands of civilians perished in the fighting or committed suicide.

ABOVE Marines of the Second Battalion, Twenty-ninth Marines, Sixth Division flush out Japanese resisters on the Oroku Peninsula at the far southwest of the island on 27 June 1945, shortly before the island was declared secured. The Japanese soldier standing is holding a white flag, an unusual act among Japanese troops, most of whom fought to the death on the island.

JULY 1944–MAY 1945

LIBERATION OF THE CAMPS

When the Allies finally advanced towards the German homeland, they began to uncover clear evidence of the atrocious nature of the regime Hitler's Germany had imposed on political prisoners, on so-called "asocials" (vagrants, the workshy, homosexuals, recidivist criminals etc.), on Gypsies and above all on the Jews of Europe. These many groups had been transported to one of a number of different kinds of camp. By 1944, there were 20 major concentration camps, with 165 sub-camps. Here, prisoners were expected to work in difficult conditions. The death rate was exceptionally high, from disease and malnutrition as much as deliberate murder, but the object was to make the prisoners labour. There were also seven main extermination camps – where Jews and other prisoners were sent for immediate murder in purpose-built centres with gas chambers and crematoria – at Majdanek, Sobibor, Chelmno, Belzec, Treblinka, Auschwitz-Birkenau (by far the largest) and a smaller facility at Maly Trostenets. At least 3.5 million people died in these camps. Majdanek and Auschwitz also served as concentration camps.

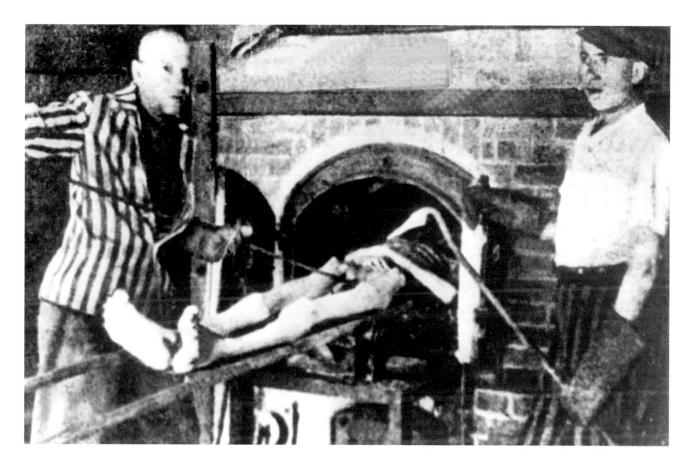

hese two, Auschwitz and Majdanek, were the first major camps to be liberated, both uncovered by the Red Army as it marched through Poland. In Majdanek in July 1944, the Red Army found 1,000 emaciated prisoners and warehouses full of hair, cases, clothing and children's toys. Auschwitz-Birkenau, half slave camp, half extermination centre, was occupied on 27 January 1945 after many of the prisoners had been forced to leave on foot 10 days earlier on one of the many "death marches" of the last months of war. Here, the Soviet soldiers found around 3,000 prisoners in the main camp, many close to death. They also found more evidence of German scrupulousness – stores of 380,000 men's suits and 836,000 women's coats and dresses, and 7.7 tons of human hair, packed

OPPOSITE Some of the female prisoners at Auschwitz shortly after their liberation by the Red Army in late January 1945. Mainly the sick or disabled remained after thousands of other prisoners were marched westwards to other camps. Soviet inmates were then interrogated by Soviet counter-intelligence in the buildings of the camp.

ABOVE Jewish prisoners at a German concentration camp demonstrate to the liberating forces how the bodies were loaded into the crematorium ovens for disposal. The gruesome work was carried out by a work detail taken from the prison population. By the end of the war most of the dead were victims of starvation and disease.

RIGHT The former commandant of Auschwitz is handed over on 25 May 1946 at Nuremberg airport to Polish policemen to stand trial in Krakow.

RUDOLF HÖSS
(1900–47)

Rudolf Höss was the notorious commandant of the Auschwitz-Birkenau complex for much of the war period. From a strict Catholic Bavarian family, he was destined at first for the priesthood, but turned against religion and joined the German army at the age of only 15. He fought in Turkey, Iraq and Palestine and, at 17, became the youngest German NCO. He served in the Freikorps after the war, became a member of the National Socialist Party in 1922, and joined the SS in 1933. He took over duties as a block commander in Dachau Concentration Camp and stayed in camp administration thereafter. He took over a camp for Polish POWs and political prisoners at Auschwitz in May 1940, and remained its commandant as it was turned into an extermination camp. He left the camp in late 1943, but returned to supervise the killing of Hungarian Jews in 1944. After the war he hid away disguised as a farmer, but was caught in March 1946 and handed over to the Polish authorities in May. He was tried, sentenced to death and then executed at the camp where he had helped to murder at least one million people.

LEFT Former SS camp guards at
Bergen-Belsen take a break from
clearing the bodies of the dead in the
camp in April 1945. As a punishment
they have been made to lie face-down in
one of the empty mass graves excavated
at the camp.

and ready to transport. But the other evidence of mass killings had been destroyed and the crematoria ovens blown up. The true horror of the camp was revealed by Soviet prisoners found there, who were interrogated by SMERSH, the military security organization, in the same buildings where they had been prisoners shortly before. The Soviet authorities had allowed some visits to Majdanek by foreign representatives, but the liberation of Auschwitz was not announced until 7 May, after the German surrender.

In the West, no extermination camps were uncovered, for these had been built on occupied Polish or Belorussian territory. British Commonwealth and American forces came across concentration camps instead, where by April 1945 conditions were lethal in the extreme. Lack of food, the absence of any form of hygiene or effective medical care, coupled with the growing brutality of the guards as the war drew to a close, created conditions in which huge numbers of prisoners died. As the German boundaries contracted, thousands of prisoners were marched from overrun camps to the few that remained in operation. It was this final migration of prisoners that caused the terrible scenes found by the British 8th Corps when units entered the camp at Bergen-Belsen in northwestern Germany on 15 April 1945. The camp had held 15,000 prisoners in December 1944, but by April there were between 40,000 and 50,000, many of them Jews forced to march on foot to the camp from sites further east. The piles of corpses and the hollow-eyed, starving prisoners became the standard images of German atrocity and were sent to newspapers in the West immediately after liberation.

The prisoners in Bergen-Belsen, where the camp was infected with typhus, continued to die in large numbers after liberation. In the end 14,000 of the 40,000 prisoners died. German civilians from the locality were brought in to view the camp on 24 April 1945, and it was burned down on British army orders in June. Further south, the American army liberated Dachau camp on 29 April. As a unit of the US 45th Division approached the camp, they found 39 rail cars filled with dead and decomposing bodies. As the soldiers approached the camp, SS guards opened fire. They were rushed by the prisoners and beaten to death. Around 70,000 prisoners were found in the Dachau system. The liberation of the camps provoked horror and outrage among the troops that first arrived on the scene, but in many cases it took years before the perpetrators were finally brought to trial.

OPPOSITE On 24 April 1945, nine days after the camp was liberated, a British army chaplain holds a brief service over a mass grave in the German concentration camp of Bergen-Belsen before it is covered over.

RIGHT A machine found in a German concentration camp near the Polish city of Lvov in 1945 used for sifting the ashes of victims whose bodies had been cremated in search of gold teeth. The gold was then boxed up and sent to Berlin.

24 JULY 1944
Red Army soldiers liberate the extermination/labour camp of Majdanek.

11 APRIL 1945
US Army liberates the Buchenwald concentration camp.

29 APRIL 1945
Dachau concentration camp is liberated by the United States Army.

4 MAY 1945
Arrest of Hans Frank, former governor general of German-occupied Poland.

23 MAY 1945
Heinrich Himmler, head of the SS and organizer of the camp system, commits suicide in British custody.

11 MARCH 1946
Rudolf Höss, disguised as a farm worker, arrested by the British.

NAZI GOLD

During the war the German state needed all the gold it could get to buy materials and equipment abroad from suppliers who would not accept payment in marks. One of the sources exploited was the gold in dental fillings taken from murdered Jews, and also from dead Soviet prisoners-of-war. The gold was packed into special containers alongside gold spectacle frames, rings and gold jewellery, and sent by rail to the German central bank in Berlin. The fillings were then melted down into ingots and transferred abroad, mainly through Swiss banks, to assist in war purchases. By the end of the war, 76 shipments had been sent from the camps, mixed in with other sources of looted gold. Only in the 1990s did the full extent of the gruesome trade become clear when a conference on Nazi gold was held in London in 1997.

JANUARY 1945–28 AUGUST 1945

VICTORY IN BURMA

After the failure of the Japanese offensive in northern India against Imphal and Kohima, Lieutenant General Slim's 14th Army began to plan the reconquest of Burma. Allied forces moved forward to the Chindwin River in western Burma, while in the north a combination of Indian forces and General Stilwell's Chinese divisions cleared the last Japanese forces and finally opened the Ledo Road (renamed at Chiang Kaishek's suggestion the Stilwell Road) in January 1945 to transport supplies to the Chinese army facing the Japanese in southern China.

S lim's plan, codenamed Operation "Capital", followed by "Extended Capital", was to drive across the Chindwin into the central Shwebo Plain, across the River Irrawaddy and on to the Burmese capital of Rangoon (Yangon). This operation involved first capturing Akyab on the coast of the Bay of Bengal, which could be used as an air base. A mixed British-Indian force captured the town on 4 January and moved on down the coast, driving the Japanese 28th Army towards the Arakan Mountains. In the central plain, Slim's forces captured Shwebo by 8 January, but then faced growing Japanese resistance from the Japanese 33rd Army stationed to defend Mandalay and the path to the south.

Slim undertook an elaborate deception plan which involved persuading the Japanese command in Burma, under Lieutenant General Hyotaro Kimura, that Mandalay was the main objective

RIGHT Airpower was a critical dimension in the Burmese campaign, not only in combat but also for essential transport and liaison operations. Here a Consolidated B-24 Liberator bomber takes part in a joint RAF/USAAF attack on Japanese stores in the Rangoon area on 17 March 1945.

OPPOSITE American-built Sherman tanks and trucks of the 62nd Indian Infantry Brigade drive along a road in March 1945 between the bridgehead over the Irrawaddy River at Nyaungyu and the key communications centre at the town of Meiktila, captured on 3 March.

4 MARCH 1945
The Philippine capital Manila falls to the US Sixth Army.

8 MAY 1945
German unconditional surrender signed in Berlin after first signing in France the day before.

13 MAY 1945
Last German resistance ends in Czechoslovakia.

6 JUNE 1945
Brazil declares war on Japan.

22 JUNE 1945
Resistance ends on the Japanese island of Okinawa after three months of fighting.

21 AUGUST 1945
Japanese Kwantung Army in Manchuria surrenders to the Red Army.

Indians of the 6/7 Rajput Regiment mop up remaining Japanese resistance in Pyawbwe, north of Rangoon on 11 April 1945. The Burmese capital was occupied by 5 May as the Japanese army withdrew eastwards.

ABOVE A wounded West African soldier of the 82nd West African Division is carried from a Stinson L-5 Sentinal aircraft at a landing strip near Kantha in February 1945. One East African and two West African divisions took part in the fighting around the Arakan Mountains in Burma.

MAJOR GENERAL AUNG SAN
(1915–47)

Aung San was the leading figure in the Burmese independence movement. He attended Rangoon (Yangon) University where he helped to organize student strikes. Strongly anti-British, he joined the nationalist Our Burma Union and became general secretary until 1940. That year, to avoid arrest, he fled to China, where he was caught by the Japanese and persuaded to go to Japan. In Bangkok, in December 1941, he set up the Burma Independence Army with Japanese support and became its first chief-of-staff. When it moved to Burma after the Japanese conquest it was renamed the Burma Defence Army and later, when Burma was granted "independence" by the Japanese in August 1943, the Burma National Army. In March 1945, he changed sides and helped the British drive out the Japanese. He became a key figure in negotiating Burmese independence, but was assassinated six months before the transfer of power by a rival political group. His daughter, Aung San Suu Kyi, went on to lead the pro-democracy movement in modern Burma (Myanmar).

for the northern Allied force, while the rest of 4th Corps went south through the mountains to outflank the Japanese and cross the Irrawaddy at Pakokku. The strategy worked almost perfectly. Against light resistance, the British and Indian forces crossed the river further south and drove for the communications centre at Meiktila, where a fierce battle took place against the Japanese 15th Army commanded by Lieutenant General Shihachi Katamura. The Japanese were caught between two forces and were not strong enough to contain both. Mandalay fell on 20 March to the northern forces, while positions around Meiktila, briefly surrounded and besieged by the Japanese, were abandoned on 29 March. There was now little between Slim's force and the city of Rangoon further to the south.

Two separate attacks were made towards the capital, one led by Lieutenant General Stopford down the Irrawaddy valley, and the other by Lieutenant General Messervy along the Sittang river. His flank was protected by the Burma Independence Army of Aung San, which changed sides in March to help end Japanese domination in Burma. Slim was anxious that Rangoon should be captured before the onset of the monsoon rains in May, and in order to be certain of it he organized a further operation, codenamed "Dracula", for the 26th Indian Division on the Arakan Coast to be taken by ship to the coast below Rangoon to take it from the sea. When the division arrived on 3 May, the Japanese had already abandoned the struggle and retreated east across the Sittang river. The forces from the north met up with the southern invasion force on 5 May and the whole of central Burma was in Allied hands.

The Japanese army was never defeated entirely in Burma. The 28th Army in the hills of Arakan tried in July 1945 to break out eastwards from its encirclement. Forewarned by intelligence sources, the British Commonwealth forces imposed 17,000 casualties at the cost of only 95 of their own. Intermittent fighting continued along the Sittang river until

LIEUTENANT GENERAL FRANK MESSERVY
(1893–1974)

A career Indian Army officer, who joined the army in 1913, Frank Messervy played a key part in the reconquest of Burma. He fought in the First World War in France, Syria and Palestine, and in the Second World War was posted to East Africa, where he commanded Gazelle Force, a fast-moving reconnaissance and strike force to support the campaign against Italian forces. In the desert war, he was the only Indian Army officer to command a British division, initially 1st Armoured then 7th Armoured. He was a poor tank commander and returned to India in 1943, where he played a part in the battles at Imphal and Kohima before taking command of the 4th Corps for the invasion in Burma in 1945, entering Rangoon in May. He was nicknamed "bearded man" because he chose not to shave during battle. After the war, he became briefly commander-in-chief of the Pakistan Army on independence in 1947, but retired in 1948.

on 28 August the Japanese surrendered formally in Rangoon. The whole operation to reconquer Burma cost only 3,188 Allied dead; Japanese dead totalled 23,000. Throughout the Burma campaign, the great weight of responsibility had fallen on the Indian Army and some 17,000 Indians lost their lives between 1941 and 1945 in what was the longest single British and Commonwealth land campaign of the war.

LEFT Indian engineers construct a wooden bridge over a shallow stream during the advance southwards from Meiktila to Rangoon. The final drive against the Japanese down the Irrawaddy and Sittang valleys was carried out by four Indian divisions.

OPPOSITE Men of the 2nd York and Lancaster Regiment search the ruins of a railway station for Japanese snipers during the advance of the 14th Army to Rangoon along the railway corridor, 13 April 1945.

1 APRIL–2 MAY 1945

VICTORY IN ITALY

As a result of the winter weather and the diversion of resources to other fronts, the campaign in Italy did not begin again until spring 1945. Allied forces amounted to 17 well-resourced divisions (British, American, Polish, Brazilian, South African, Indian and the New Zealand Division) and substantial airpower. Kesselring, who was replaced in March by Colonel General von Vietinghoff, had 23 divisions, most very under-strength, with an average of 1,700 soldiers in each, little air power and the assistance of two Italian divisions of Marshal Graziani's Army of Liguria, all that was left of the Fascist armed forces.

Alexander planned a major campaign to complete the destruction of Axis forces. Operation "Grapeshot" aimed to encircle the German 14th and 10th armies south of the River Po, almost all of whose bridges had been destroyed long before by Allied air power. The US Fifth Army would attack west of Bologna and then swing eastwards, while the British 8th Army under Lieutenant General McCreery was to force the Argenta Gap on the coast and then swing westwards. After a number of small preliminary operations to tidy up the Allied line, the operation was launched on 9 April when waves of heavy bombers, followed by 200 medium bombers and 500 fighter-bombers, attacked the German line.

16 APRIL 1945
Launch of the Red Army's major campaign against Berlin by Konev's 1st Ukrainian and Zhukov's 2nd Belorussian army groups.

20 APRIL 1945
US forces enter the Bavarian city of Nuremberg, where the prewar Nazi Party rallies were staged.

25 APRIL 1945
Opening of the San Francisco Conference for founding of the United Nations.

1 MAY 1945
New German government under Grand Admiral Dönitz following Hitler's suicide the day before.

5 MAY 1945
German forces surrender in Norway.

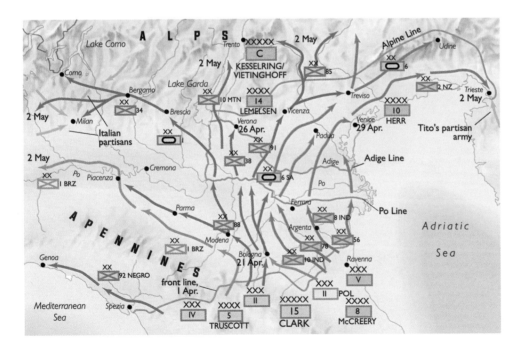

LEFT Victory in Italy, 1 April–2 May 1945.

OPPOSITE A British Churchill Crocodile flamethrower tank supports infantry of the 2nd New Zealand Division during the assault across the Senio River south of Ravenna on 9 April 1945, at the start of the final campaign in northern Italy.

GENERAL RICHARD MCCREERY
(1898–1967)

Richard McCreery was commander of the British 8th Army in its last years in the Italian campaign. He joined the army in 1915 and served for most of the First World War in France with the 12th Royal Lancers, whose commander he became in the 1930s. He commanded the 2nd Armoured Brigade in the Battle of France, then moved to North Africa as adviser on armoured vehicles and then Chief-of-Staff, 18th Army Group. He was posted to Italy in July 1943 to command 10th Corps, and towards the end of 1944 took over command of the 8th Army from Lieutenant General Leese. He led it to a famous victory over German forces in the Po Valley. After the war he commanded occupation troops in Austria, and in 1946 became Commander-in-Chief of the British Army of the Rhine. He retired from the army in 1949 with the rank of general.

LIEUTENANT GENERAL KARL WOLFF
(1900–84)

Karl Wolff was a high-ranking SS man who negotiated the armistice on the Italian front in the spring of 1945. He joined the army in 1917 and saw action on the Western Front, but was demobilized after the war. He became a businessman in the 1920s, but during the slump of 1929–32 he became convinced that only radical politics held the answer. He joined the National Socialist Party in 1931 and the SS the same year. He joined Himmler's staff and by 1935 was chief of the personal staff of the Reichsführer-SS. He became the SS representative at Hitler's headquarters, and in July 1943 was sent to Italy as supreme SS representative. It was here that he began secret negotiations for an armistice in February 1945, which led to an end of hostilities on 2 May. He was arrested and served several short periods of imprisonment before being sentenced by a West German court to 15 years in jail in 1964. On account of poor health, he was released in 1971.

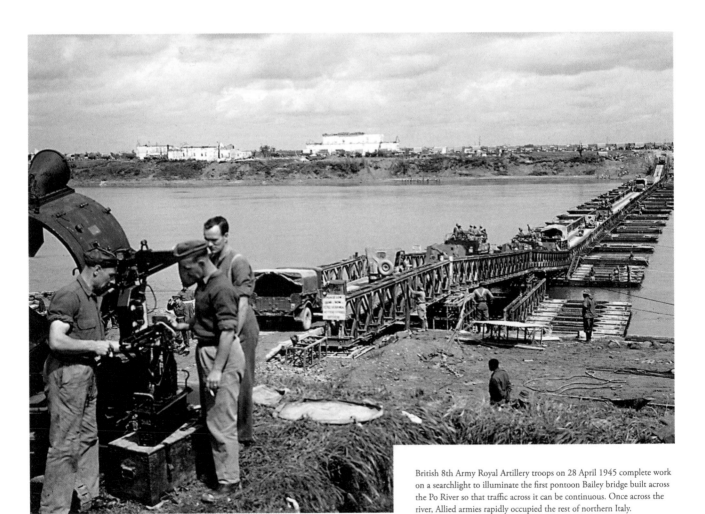

British 8th Army Royal Artillery troops on 28 April 1945 complete work on a searchlight to illuminate the first pontoon Bailey bridge built across the Po River so that traffic across it can be continuous. Once across the river, Allied armies rapidly occupied the rest of northern Italy.

BOMBACCI GELORMINI MUSSOLINI PETACCI PAVOLINI STARACE

The corpse of the Italian dictator Benito Mussolini (centre) hangs upside down next to his mistress, Clara Petacci, shot by partisans while trying to escape to Switzerland on 28 April 1945. Other Fascist leaders were killed at the same time and hung up in Piazzale Loreto next to their dead leader.

Already dispirited, and with German commanders trying to negotiate a secret armistice, the German army crumbled quickly and by 17 April Argenta was captured and the way opened to exploit westwards and north towards Venice.

The US Fifth Army opened its part of the offensive on 14 April, moving quickly through the mountains and reaching the outskirts of Bologna by 20 April. Hitler refused von Vietinghoff's request to withdraw and growing numbers of German prisoners were taken as Bologna was encircled by the two Allied armies, who met on 25 April at Finale nell'Emilia. The Po valley provided a much easier battlefield, and with little serious opposition remaining the US Fifth Army reached Verona on 26 April, swinging west to take Milan. The 8th Army moved rapidly north, crossing the Po unopposed on 24 April, liberating Venice on 29 April and reaching Trieste on 2 May, just after the arrival of Tito's forces. A German delegation arrived at Alexander's headquarters at Caserta on 28 April and an armistice was agreed the next day to come into effect on 2 May.

On 27 April Mussolini, still nominal head of the Italian Social Republic, and his mistress Clara Petacci were caught by partisans of the Garibaldi Brigade at Dongo at the head of Lake Como as they made an unsuccessful

bid to escape to Switzerland. Mussolini, Clara and other Fascist leaders were executed, their bodies taken to Milan and hung upside down in Piazzale Loreto, where Italian partisans had been murdered some time before. All over northern Italy, cities were liberated by partisan groups even before the arrival of Allied forces. In Milan, on 26 April, the local partisans established their own government before the Americans arrived. What followed was a period of great confusion as the pro-Allied Italian government in Rome tried to co-operate with partisan groups, many of whom were Communists distrustful of other Italian political groups. A coalition was formed in June 1945 under the democrat and anti-Fascist Feruccio Parri which brought together all the groups involved in the struggle to liberate Italy from German rule.

The cost of the long campaign in Italy was very high. The US Fifth Army suffered 188,746 casualties, the 8th Army 123,993. German casualties amounted to at least 435,000. Around 60,000 Italians were killed by bombing attacks, most of them in the last year of the war. The war and the bombing destroyed important parts of Italy's cultural heritage while the divisions between Fascists and partisans left a long residue of bitterness and hostility in Italian society and politics.

BATTLE FOR BERLIN

The end of the massive Vistula-Oder operation left the Red Army only 65 kilometres (40 miles) from Berlin by the beginning of February 1945. But the drive for the capital, first planned the previous November, had to be postponed because of Stalin's anxiety about the remaining substantial pockets of German resistance in Königsberg, Breslau, Poznan and the fortress of Küstrin. Further north in Pomerania, scattered German units were gathered together under Army Group Vistula, briefly commanded by the head of the SS, Heinrich Himmler. Stalin also worried about the intentions of his Western allies, who were rapidly crossing Germany from the west, and his fears were only allayed when Eisenhower finally told him in March that he would move southeast and north, leaving Berlin to the Red Army.

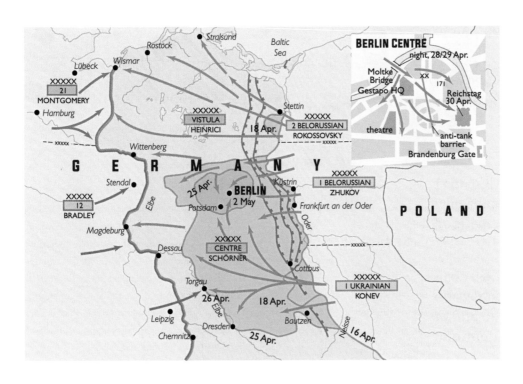

Berlin, 19 April–7 May 1945

——— front lines, with date

▃▃▃ defensive lines

18 APRIL 1945

Field Marshal Model surrenders 225,000 soldiers trapped in the Ruhr pocket, then kills himself.

3 MAY 1945

The German port city of Hamburg is captured by the British 21st Army Group.

The German strongpoints were gradually reduced during February and March, but the fortress at Küstrin, besieged by General Chuikov's 8th Guards Army, was only captured on 29 March. Rokossovsky's 2nd Belorussian Army Group reached Danzig, on the Baltic coast, a day later. Detailed planning for the final Berlin operation began in mid-March. Stalin was keen that the final operation should be a clear success, since it would take place in full view of his allies. Over two million men, in 29 armies, supported by 3,155 tanks and 7,500 aircraft, crowded into a wide semi-circle around the German capital. Opposing them were the forces of Army Group Centre under General Ferdinand Schörner and Army Group Vistula, now under General Gotthard Heinrici, which together could muster around one million men, many of them irregulars of the recently-created Volkssturm made up of over-age men and boys. They could muster 1,519 tanks and very few aircraft.

The battle plan was for a frontal assault on Berlin by Zhukov's 1st Belorussian Army Group across the Seelow Heights on the far bank of

LIEUTENANT GENERAL HELMUTH WEIDLING
(1891–1955)

Helmuth Weidling was the last commander of the Berlin Defence District, and surrendered the city to the Red Army on 2 May. He joined the army in 1911, and served as an artillery commander in the early stages of the Second World War. He then commanded the 41st Tank Corps in the Soviet Union, rising by 1943 to the rank of general of artillery. In April 1945, he was appointed commander of the 56th Tank Corps facing the Soviet campaign against Berlin. He was condemned to death by Hitler for withdrawing his force, but reprieved just before his execution after the reasons for the retreat were explained. On 23 April, he was appointed defender of Berlin and negotiated its surrender with General Chuikov on 2 May. "I think every unnecessary death is a crime," he told Chuikov. He was arrested and died in a Soviet prison in 1955 during a 25-year sentence for failing to surrender Berlin sooner.

LEFT Armshield worn by volunteers from Turkistan serving with the German army.

BELOW On 3 April 1945 German grenadiers lie in wait on the Seelow Heights above the Oder river in small pits from where they will oppose the Soviet bridgehead over the river using the Panzerfaust hand-held anti-tank weapons. The attack came 13 days later.

RED FLAG OVER THE REICHSTAG

The photograph taken by the Soviet photographer Yevgeni Khaldei of the Red Flag flying over the Reichstag, the German parliament building, in May 1945 is one of the most famous pictures of the war. The story behind the flag is nonetheless confusing. The first Red Flag was raised at approximately 10.40 p.m. on the evening of 30 April after a small group of Soviet soldiers fought their way to the roof and placed the Red Banner of the 3rd Shock Army on one of the statues. The flag was photographed by a Russian aircraft the following day before German fire dislodged it. It was retrieved two days later and in June sent to Moscow. Khaldei's flag was made from three red tablecloths, allegedly sewn with the hammer and sickle by his uncle, which he took to Berlin and then had hoisted onto the roof on 2 May by two soldiers, after the Germans in the building had surrendered. This photograph had to be doctored to remove the two watches on the soldiers' wrists and to add more smoke in the background, but it remains among the most heavily used images of the European war.

the Oder straight towards the heart of Berlin while some units swept westwards, encircling the city; in the south Konev's 1st Ukrainian Army Group, which had fought a draining campaign to pacify Silesia, was to attack towards the Elbe with orders to swing northwards towards Zhukov if help were needed or asked for; in the north Rokossovsky would clear

LEFT A dead German soldier lies on the roadside in the battle for Berlin in late April 1945. Although the German army had few resources left to defend the city, the Soviet forces sustained heavy casualties.

German resistance to ensure that Zhukov's flank was secure. On 1 April, Stalin summoned the commanders to a conference where he asked, "Well, who is going to take Berlin?" Although the honour was supposed to be Zhukov's, Stalin left it open, in case circumstances changed on the battlefield and Konev could move faster.

As the campaign unfolded, it became clear that Zhukov might be beaten to the target by Konev. The assault on the Seelow Heights, even with overwhelming strength, proved one of Zhukov's few disasters. On the morning of 16 April, he sent his forces forward for a direct assault on the hills, crammed in a narrow salient, bombarded endlessly by hidden German defences. Caught in swampy ground, and dazzled by Soviet searchlights which reflected back from the accumulated smoke of battle

on to advancing Soviet soldiers, Zhukov's forces took more than two days to clear the Heights, and then found a third defensive zone lying just beyond. Only by 20 April did the advance units of Chuikov's 8th Guards Army, part of Zhukov's army group, reach the eastern suburbs of Berlin and begin the bombardment of the central areas. North of the city, the remnants of Heinrici's Army Group Vistula crumbled and Zhukov's armies swept round Berlin to encircle it.

On the morning of 25 April, the first of Zhukov's units crossed the River Spree, close to the centre of the city. When Chuikov's army approached Schönefeld airfield they were met not by Germans but by forward units of Konev's 3rd Tank Army. While Zhukov had struggled to reach the capital, Konev's armies had swept easily through eastern

Germany into Saxony so that Konev was free to order some of his army to march northwards and attack Berlin from the south. After the first encounter, Chuikov deliberately drove for the centre of Berlin across the path of Konev's forces. Konev bowed to reality and allowed Zhukov to seize the prize. By 29 April, Chuikov began to storm the Tiergarten, west of the government zone, and on 30 April the first units fought their way into the Reichstag building. German resistance, at times fanatical and suicidal, crumbled away. Two days later, the remains of the Berlin garrison surrendered. The final campaign for the city cost the Soviet forces 78,000 dead; German losses have always been difficult to calculate, but are believed to run into hundreds of thousands for the last weeks of fighting.

ABOVE A Volkssturmgewehr VG-1-5 rifle used by members of the Volkssturm.

BELOW German prisoners of war are marched through the Brandenburg Gate past a JS-II tank on their way to captivity on 2 May 1945. The last prisoners returned to Germany in 1955.

7–11 MAY 1945

THE GERMAN SURRENDER

The final surrender of remaining Axis forces in Europe was an uncoordinated and messy process. Though victory in Europe was proclaimed on 8 May, resistance still continued in some parts, while the Soviet Union announced victory on 9 May and declared 11 May as a day of celebration. Even the formal signing of a surrender document had to be done twice to satisfy Soviet sensibilities.

The first surrender came in Italy where a ceasefire, signed by General Heinrich von Vietinghoff on 29 April, came into effect on 2 May, the same day as the surrender in Berlin. Some 490,000 German and Axis soldiers were taken prisoner. The surrender of forces in Germany and Austria took place as each area was encircled or captured. On 4 May, German forces in northern Germany and the Netherlands surrendered to Field Marshal Montgomery's 21st Army Group; on 5 May German forces in Bavaria surrendered. Also on 5 May, the new German government in Flensburg ordered Hitler's wartime chief of operations, General Alfred Jodl, to proceed to the French city of Rheims to surrender to the Western Allies, still hoping perhaps that a division could be opened up between the West and Stalin. Eisenhower insisted on unconditional German surrender, as had been the case in all the subsidiary theatres. At 2.40 in the early morning of 7 May, a brief ceremony took place in a schoolhouse in Rheims, which Eisenhower had made his temporary headquarters. Surrounded by Allied officers and 17 invited newsmen, Jodl signed the act of surrender. The Soviet representative, General Susloparov, caught unawares by the capitulation and uncertain about what his instructions from Moscow would be, signed in a way that suggested the possibility of a second ceremony. A little later a directive from Stalin arrived ordering him to sign nothing.

Stalin deeply distrusted his Allies for agreeing to a full German surrender without proper Soviet participation. At a meeting in the Kremlin that night he accused the West of organizing a "shady deal" with the defeated Germans. He refused to accept the Rheims document and pressed his allies to agree to a formal, public ceremony in Berlin, the heart of the

RIGHT Air Chief Marshal Sir Arthur Tedder, deputy supreme Allied commander to Eisenhower at SHAEF, signs the German unconditional surrender document at Soviet headquarters in Berlin during the second surrender ceremony held on 8 May to satisfy Stalin.

OPPOSITE Crowds in New York's Times Square on 42nd Street celebrate VE Day on 8 May 1945 overlooked by a giant model figure of the Statue of Liberty.

FIELD MARSHAL WILHELM KEITEL
(1883–1946)

Wilhelm Keitel, nicknamed "Lakaitel" (lackey) by his critics, was chief-of-staff at Supreme Headquarters. He joined the army in 1901, and served in the Field Artillery in 1914 until severely wounded. He served the rest of the war in staff positions and in 1919–20 helped to organize Freikorps activity against Poland. From 1924, he became a senior administrator in the army and in 1935, as a lieutenant general, was promoted to run the Armed Forces Office in the War Ministry. When the ministry was replaced in February 1938 by the Supreme Headquarters, directly under Hitler's control, Keitel continued his job as the senior administrator, now designated "chief-of-staff", and ran the headquarters from then until the end of the war. Though he did not always approve of what Hitler planned, Keitel earned his nickname by following orders. He signed numerous documents on Hitler's behalf, including the notorious "commissar order" for murdering Soviet commissars attached to the Red Army. He was arrested in May 1945, tried at Nuremberg and hanged on 16 October 1945.

enemy war effort. His allies agreed and a second surrender document was prepared in Moscow, which had to be reconciled during the course of 8 May with the Western version. A power failure left the typists completing the draft by candlelight. Exactly at the stroke of midnight, Field Marshal Keitel led the German delegation into the room in the former German military engineering school. He signed for the Germans, Marshal Zhukov for the Soviet Union, Air Chief Marshal Arthur Tedder for the British Empire, General Carl Spaatz for the Americans and General de Lattre de Tassigny for the French.

By this time the British and American people had already been told about the surrender and 8 May was designated Victory in Europe (VE) Day and a public holiday. Scenes of jubilation, widely photographed in London, were more modest in other parts of the country. During the course of the day, Churchill appeared next to the royal family on the balcony at Buckingham Palace to an ecstatic welcome. The Soviet population were only told about the surrender early in the morning of 9 May, and only two days later was there a formal day of celebration. In central Europe Soviet forces were still fighting against the remnants of Field Marshal Schörner's Army Group Centre, which had retreated for a last stand in Czechoslovakia. It was overwhelmed by Konev's 1st Ukrainian Army Group and Malinovsky's 2nd Ukrainian Army Group and finally surrendered on 11–12 May 1945. Elsewhere, news of the surrender was brought to German garrisons in Lorient and St Nazaire on the French Atlantic coast, in the Channel Islands and at the port of Dunkirk, which had all been bypassed in earlier campaigns and never freed. Local documents of surrender had to be signed in Denmark and Norway. It had taken almost a week from Jodl's original instructions for the cumbersome process of unconditional surrender to be completed.

THE FLENSBURG REGIME

After the suicide of Hitler and Goebbels in the bunker, the government of Germany was temporarily assumed by Grand Admiral Karl Dönitz, Hitler's appointed successor as Reich president. Dönitz had his headquarters at Flensburg near the Danish border and for two weeks after the end of the war was allowed to operate freely, with a cabinet of ministers and a small defence force. The government in reality ruled nothing, but did authorize the German surrender on 7 May and the second surrender in Berlin a day later. There was some confusion among the Allied powers as to what to do with the new regime, which hoped to become a German provisional government. In the end, on 23 May, a unit of British soldiers was sent to Flensburg and arrested the whole government, except for the former minister Himmler, who was caught a day earlier and committed suicide after he was recognized.

LEFT Grand Admiral Karl Dönitz leads the remnants of the German government in Flensburg following their arrest by British soldiers on 23 May 1945. Behind him are Albert Speer and Alfred Jodl.

INSTRUMENT OF GERMAN SURRENDER

The instrument of surrender of German forces in the Netherlands, Denmark and northwest Germany, signed by Montgomery for the Allies and five German commanders, headed by Admiral Hans von Friedeburg, who had been appointed German navy commander-in-chief the previous day.

2 MAY
Axis forces in Italy surrender unconditionally.

4 MAY 1945
German forces surrender in northern Germany and the Netherlands.

6 MAY 1945
The 82-day Soviet siege of Breslau comes to an end.

7 MAY 1945
German submarine U-2336 sinks last two merchantmen of the war.

8 MAY 1945
Reich Marshal Hermann Göring gives himself up to the Americans, the highest-ranking German prisoner.

Instrument of Surrender

of

All German armed forces in HOLLAND, in

northwest Germany including all islands,

and in DENMARK.

1. The German Command agrees to the surrender of all German armed forces in HOLLAND, in northwest GERMANY including the FRISIAN ISLANDS and HELIGOLAND and all other islands, in SCHLESWIG-HOLSTEIN, and in DENMARK, to the C.-in-C. 21 Army Group. *This to include all naval ships in these areas.* These forces to lay down their arms and to surrender unconditionally.

2. All hostilities on land, on sea, or in the air by German forces in the above areas to cease at 0800 hrs. British Double Summer Time on Saturday 5 May 1945.

3. The German command to carry out at once, and without argument or comment, all further orders that will be issued by the Allied Powers on any subject.

4. Disobedience of orders, or failure to comply with them, will be regarded as a breach of these surrender terms and will be dealt with by the Allied Powers in accordance with the accepted laws and usages of war.

5. This instrument of surrender is independent of, without prejudice to, and will be superseded by any general instrument of surrender imposed by or on behalf of the Allied Powers and applicable to Germany and the German armed forces as a whole.

6. This instrument of surrender is written in English and in German.

   The English version is the authentic text.

7. The decision of the Allied Powers will be final if any doubt or dispute arises as to the meaning or interpretation of the surrender terms.

Friedeburg

Kinzel.

E. Wagner

B. L. Montgomery
Field-Marshal

4 May 1945
1830 hrs

6–9 AUGUST 1945

THE ATOMIC BOMBS

The final defeat of Japan was long expected to be a costly and lengthy campaign and the determination with which the Japanese forces defended Iwo Jima and Okinawa reinforced this conviction. A campaign plan for what was called Operation "Olympic" was drawn up, but unofficial estimates suggested that there would be between 500,000 and one million American casualties in an invasion of the home islands, and although military chiefs thought this exaggerated, they knew that Japan would be defended with more than usual ferocity. The sea blockade and the bombing of Japan's cities would, it was hoped, produce the defeat of Japan without a full invasion.

It is against this background that the decision to use the atomic bomb was made. Since 1942, under the codename of the "Manhattan Project", a large team of scientists in the United States had worked to produce a useable bomb. The physics necessary to understand how a bomb might be developed and what its possible effects would be was pioneered in the 1930s, and by 1939 the theoretical feasibility of such a bomb was established. The problem lay with production. In 1940, a high-level committee of scientists in Britain, known as the Maud Committee, was set up to report on the bomb. In July 1941 the committee concluded that a bomb could be made in the probable period of the war from enriched uranium and in October Churchill's government gave the go-ahead. The British did not recommend using plutonium, a new element derived from uranium, but this was developed later in the United States and used for one of the bombs.

The economic effort of making the bomb proved beyond British capabilities, and in June 1942 the United States took over full responsibility for the whole project. British scientists moved to America and worked with a scientific team under Robert Oppenheimer. The whole project cost $2 billion and employed 600,000 people, and by the summer of 1945 enough plutonium and bomb-grade uranium-235 had been produced to test and use atomic weapons. On 16 July 1945, at the Alamogordo air base in New Mexico, a plutonium bomb was detonated successfully. News of the explosion was sent to Roosevelt's successor President Truman, who was attending the inter-Allied conference at Potsdam. He approved the use of two bombs on Japanese cities. Whether this decision was taken principally to avoid an invasion of Japan, or to test the new technology or to impress the Soviet Union, has been argued over ever since.

OPPOSITE An aerial view of the atomic attack on Hiroshima, 6 August 1945.

ROBERT OPPENHEIMER
(1904–67)

Robert Oppenheimer was the physicist who led the research on the atomic bomb as scientific director at the laboratory at Los Alamos. The son of a textile merchant, Oppenheimer was marked out from an early age as a scholar and intellectual of extraordinary power and range. He studied theoretical physics in Germany in the 1920s before returning to America as professor of physics at Berkeley, California. It was his pioneering work on nuclear research in the United States together with his charismatic personality and driving energy that made him a natural choice to run the scientific side of the Manhattan Project. His flirtation with American Communism did not prevent his work at the time, but after the war, as chairman of the General Advisory Committee of the Atomic Energy Commission, he made powerful enemies who disliked his radicalism. In 1954, his security status was revoked when he was investigated by Senator McCarthy's UnAmerican Activities Committee. He moved to Princeton as director of the Institute of Advanced Study and died of throat cancer in 1967.

19 JULY 1945
600 B-29 bombers drop 4,000 tons of bombs on Japan in a single raid.

28 JULY 1945
Last US ship sunk by a *kamikaze* plane off Okinawa.

30 JULY 1945
The USS *Indianapolis* is sunk by a Japanese submarine after delivering vital parts for the atomic bombs at Tinian island.

2 AUGUST 1945
6,600 tons of bombs, the highest wartime total, dropped on Japanese cities.

9 AUGUST 1945
President Truman ratifies the United Nations Charter, making the USA the first state to do so.

LIEUTENANT GENERAL LESLIE GROVES
(1896–1970)

Leslie Groves is best remembered for two things. He was a senior military engineer who supervised the construction of the Pentagon building in Washington, and also military head of the Manhattan Project for constructing the atomic bomb. He joined the army in 1918 after education at the Massachusetts Institute of Technology, and became an officer in the US Corps of Engineers. In 1940, promoted to lieutenant colonel, he joined the General Staff as chief of operations, Corps of Engineers, and deputy to the chief of construction. He was an energetic and ruthless administrator who played a major part in organizing the huge construction projects made necessary by the expansion of the US military between 1940 and 1942. In September 1942, he was appointed as military director of the bomb project which he codenamed "Manhattan". He was one of the leading advocates of bombing the ancient Japanese capital of Kyoto, but was overruled. He retired in 1948 with the rank of lieutenant general, unhappy about the transfer of the nuclear programme to the civilian Atomic Energy Commission.

Some Japanese cities had not been bombed by LeMay's Twenty-first Bomber Command so the atomic weapons could be tried out on them. The first bomb was used against Hiroshima on the morning of 6 August 1945. Nicknamed "Little Boy", the 4,000-kilogram (8,800-pound) uranium bomb was carried in a B-29 bomber from Tinian. It caught Hiroshima's workforce on its way to work. Thirteen square kilometres (five square miles) were utterly destroyed and an estimated 120,000 about 40 per cent of the city's population died either immediately or within a few days from the effects of radiation. The second bomb, carried from Tinian on the morning of 9 August, was destined for the city of Kokura but it was obscured by cloud and the crew dropped the 4,600-kilogram (10,200-pound) plutonium bomb – dubbed "Fat Man" – on the secondary target, Nagasaki. The city was sheltered by hills and the blast effects less damaging, but an estimated 74,000 people were killed and 74,000 injured from a population of 270,000. Tens of thousands suffered the long-term after-effects of exposure to high levels of radiation.

The effect in Japan was one of disbelief at first, turning rapidly to terror at the prospect of further attacks. In reality, the United States was not yet in a position to drop a further atomic bomb, but the same day as the Nagasaki attack the Japanese prime minister asked Emperor Hirohito to decide on the issue of surrender. The effect on the Soviet Union of the atomic attacks was less startling than the Americans had hoped, since spies had already supplied extensive information on the Manhattan Project. Stalin ordered a high-speed programme of nuclear development and the Soviet Union detonated its first atomic test in August 1949, by which time the United States had a further 298 bombs.

The centre of the Japanese city of Hiroshima after the atomic bomb attack on 6 August 1945. The large building in the centre is the Industry Promotional Hall which was retained in its ruined state as a war memorial.

ABOVE The suburban Nagasaki in September 1945 after the second atomic bomb was dropped on 9 August 1945. This scene was eight kilometres (five miles) from the epicentre of the explosion.

OPPOSITE Colonel Paul Tibbets standing in front of his B-29 "Superfortress" bomber Enola Gay, which carried the first atomic bomb for the attack on Hiroshima, August 1945. He helped to train and organize the 509th Composite Group, which was to undertake the atomic attacks in the summer of 1945.

14 AUGUST–2 SEPTEMBER 1945

THE JAPANESE SURRENDER

The Allied demand for the unconditional surrender of Japan presented a more difficult process than was the case in Europe. Surrender was deeply dishonourable for the Japanese military, which was why so many Japanese soldiers and sailors fought literally until the last, or committed suicide. The military domination of decision-making in Japan and the prevailing ethos of sacrifice for the sake of the Emperor impeded any attempt by civilian leaders during 1945, faced with the inevitability of defeat, to find a formula that would satisfy both the Allies and the Japanese military.

The Japanese General Yoshijiro Umezu signs the instrument of unconditional surrender on behalf of the Japanese army aboard the battleship USS *Missouri* on 2 September 1945.

The Japanese leadership also shared many illusions about the invincibility of Japan and the defensibility of the Empire. Only with the heavy destruction of Japanese cities in 1945 and the bombardment of the homeland by Allied ships and carrier aircraft was it evident to the wider population that the propaganda of victory had been a cruel deception. Yet in the face of defeat the military decided that the Japanese homeland would be defended at all costs under the slogan "The Glorious Death of One Hundred Million". In January 1945, a Homeland Operations Plan was formulated and in March a law passed to enforce the creation of People's Volunteer Units, followed in June by the creation of People's Volunteer Combat Corps. These people's militia were poorly armed and supplied, but the assumption among Japan's military was that death must always be preferable to dishonour.

In April 1945, a new prime minister, Admiral Kantaro Suzuki, was installed. While some efforts were made to see if there was an acceptable formula for an end to hostilities, Suzuki continued to work with military plans for a final defence. On 26 July, the Allies announced the Potsdam Declaration which re-affirmed the demand for unconditional surrender and committed the Allies to the democratic reconstruction of Japan. The stumbling block remained the question of the Emperor: unless the Allies would guarantee the survival of the monarchy, the government would not be able to endorse surrender. Hirohito had already let it be known through the Japanese ambassador in Moscow (Japan and the Soviet Union were not yet at war) that Japan wished to end the war, but his own position made it difficult to deliver what the Allies wanted.

The changed circumstances of early August forced the hand of the Japanese government. On 6 August, the first atomic bomb was dropped and on 8–9 August, before the bomb on Nagasaki, Soviet forces opened up a major offensive against the Japanese Kwantung Army in Manchuria. The Soviet army expected a hard fight in difficult terrain, but so weakened was Japanese capability that the million men, 5,000 tanks and 5,000 aircraft of the Far Eastern army groups overwhelmed Japanese opposition within six days, with the deaths of 80,000 Japanese. On 9 August, Suzuki finally asked the Emperor to decide on surrender or a final fight to the death and the Emperor, who had already had secret intimations from the Americans that the throne would be protected, opted for surrender. He had to repeat his decision at an imperial conference on 14 August, and the following day – despite continued opposition from the military – he made an unprecedented broadcast to his people that Japan would surrender.

The final process proved as messy as it had been in Europe. Some Japanese soldiers continued to fight on weeks after the decision to surrender. Many could not be reached in distant outposts and garrisons and the Allied troops had great difficulty in persuading them that the surrender was actually true. In Manchuria, formal surrender came only on 21 August and fighting continued in some areas until September. On 2 September, aboard the battleship USS *Missouri* in Tokyo Bay, Japanese representatives

14 AUGUST 1945
Japanese army coup against the Emperor is frustrated by soldiers loyal to the monarchy.

15 AUGUST 1945
Victory in Japan (VJ) Day is celebrated in Allied countries.

21 AUGUST 1945
The American Lend-Lease programme is formally brought to an end.

30 AUGUST 1945
US Army and Marine units arrive on the Japanese home islands to begin the occupation.

31 AUGUST 1945
General MacArthur establishes the Supreme Allied Command in Tokyo, with control over Japan.

2 SEPTEMBER 1945
Vietnamese nationalist and Communist Ho Chi Minh declares Vietnamese independence, launching a long 30-year struggle for a united and independent Vietnam.

EMPEROR HIROHITO
(1901–89)

Hirohito came to the throne of Japan in 1926, taking the name "Showa" (enlightened peace) as the designation of his reign. He was a reserved and scholarly man, with a lifelong interest in marine biology. His reign was at first characterized by a strong pro-Western stance and Hirohito endorsed the parliamentary system which in practice restricted his own extensive prerogatives as Japan's supreme sovereign. The political system allowed Hirohito very limited room for initiative and when the military came to dominate politics in the 1930s, Hirohito was usually asked to endorse policies already approved by the army and navy. He was personally opposed to the war with China and the declaration of war on the United States, but was presented in both cases with a *fait accompli* which he could not easily reverse. He was nevertheless unwilling for Japan to abandon its empire or to accept dishonour, and as a result was a reluctant partner in the military imperialism of his cabinets. In 1945, he played a key part in finally forcing the military to accept surrender. He remained on the throne from 1945 until his death in 1989, helping to adapt Japan to modern democracy.

met with General MacArthur to sign the formal instruments of surrender. Japanese forces surrendered in China on 9 September, in Burma on 13 September and in Hong Kong on 16 September. Japan was occupied by American and British Commonwealth forces; the Emperor was not deposed, and played an important part in the democratic reconstruction of his country.

OPPOSITE Jubilant Manchurians greet the Soviet army as it enters Port Arthur on 22 August 1945 after a lightning victory over the occupying Japanese Kwantung Army. The Manchurian territory was ceded to China in 1946 and became part of the new Communist People's Republic in 1949.

ABOVE The US First Cavalry Division parading down a main street in Tokyo on 4 July 1946 during Independence Day celebrations. The commanders of the First Cavalry Division and the US Eighth Army took the march-past in front of the Imperial Hotel.

SURRENDER OF JAPAN HEADLINES

Two newspaper front pages – the *Amrita Bazar Patrika* in Calcutta and the *Daily Mail* in London – announce the surrender of Japan on 15 August 1945. A new wave of celebrations followed as Allied populations everywhere appreciated the final end of the war.

EXTRAORDINARY ISSUE

Amrita Bazar Patrika

REGD. No. C. 58.   CALCUTTA, WEDNESDAY, AUGUST 15, 1945.   Editor — TUSHAR KANTI GHOSH,   SRABAN 30, 1352, B. S.   PRICE 2 PICE.

JAPAN QUITS!

"PREPARATION FOR CIVIL WAR"

Communists' Allegations Against Chiang: Orders To Chuh Teh Condemned

NEW YORK, Aug. 14.—The Chinese Communist Radio at Yenan, as quoted by the United States Office of War Information, to-day called on the Chinese people and the Allies to support its claim that the Chinese forces in all liberated areas should participate with the Allies in receiving Japanese surrender.

It said that Generalissimo Chiang's orders to the Communist General not to take independent action was "further proof of Chiang's preference for the Japanese and their puppets to the democratic forces in his country and of his active preparation for a civil war."—(Reuter).

Gandhiji's Hint Of Impending Fast

SEWAGRAM, Aug. 14.—Mahatma Gandhi to-day speaking to Harijan workers hinted of an impending fast for him though he could not say when.

He said, "Yet another fast is in store for me but I do not know how, when and for what purpose will I start it."—(A.P.)

LONDON, Aug. 14.—Prime Minister Clement Attlee, broadcasting at midnight, said Japan has to-day surrendered.—Reuter.

Full Acceptance Of Allied Terms

WASHINGTON, Aug. 14.—President Truman states that he deems the Japanese reply as "full acceptance of the Potsdam declaration which specifies unconditional surrender of Japan."—Reuter.

TEXTILES FOR INDIA

NEW DELHI, Aug. 14.—It is learnt that with a view to affording relief in India in meeting her requirements of cotton textiles, the Government of India have arranged to obtain certain allocations of these goods from the United Kingdom and the United States of America.—(U.P.).

Japan's Reply To Allied Terms

LONDON, Aug. 13.—The Prime Minister Mr. Clement Attlee, announcing in a midnight broadcast that Japan has surrendered, gave the text of Japan's reply to the Allied terms of surrender.

It reads: "With reference to the announcement of August 10, regarding the acceptance of the provisions of the Potsdam declaration and the reply of the governments of the States, Great Britain, the Soviet Union and China, sent by Secretary of State Mr. James Byrnes on Aug. 11, the Japanese Government has the honour to reply to the governments of the Four Powers as follows:—

(1) His Majesty the Emperor has been free to forbid their ultimate form of Government.

(2) Allied troops are to remain in Japan for a specified period.

The terms were sent to the Japanese Government through Switzerland on Saturday afternoon in reply to the Japanese offer to accept the Potsdam terms on condition that the Emperor be allowed to remain.

POTSDAM TERMS

The Potsdam terms, set out in a declaration by President Truman, Mr. Winston Churchill and Generalissimo Chiang, included three conditions:

Firstly, Japanese sovereignty is to be limited to the four main home Islands and other islands to be determined by the Allies.

Secondly, Allied troops are to occupy points in the country until a new order has been established.

Thirdly, Japanese armed forces are to be disarmed and sent home.

Fourthly, Japanese war industries are to be destroyed and reparations exacted in kind.—(Reuter).

CLOTHS FOR BENGAL

Adequate Supply To Meet Pujah Demands

(From Our Own Correspondent)
NEW DELHI, Aug. 13.—The Government of India, I understand, are ensuring adequate supply of cloth to meet the Pujah demands in Bengal. Arrangements are being made to despatch large consignments of cloth which will be made available to the public before the Pujahs.

FRENCH TAKE OVER IN BERLIN

BERLIN, Aug. 14.—French occupation forces to-day took over their zone of Berlin at a formal flag raising ceremony in the Borough of Wedding. The French zone includes Wedding and Reinnendorp boroughs.—(A. P. of America.)

Allied Terms To Japan

LONDON, Aug. 14.—There were the terms Japan was asked to accept:—

(1) The Japanese Emperor and Government are to subject their authority to that of the Allied Supreme Commander, (General Douglas MacArthur has been insufficiently tipped for the post).

(2) The Japanese Emperor is to order the surrender of Japanese troops in all theatres.

(3) The Japanese Government is to transport prisoners and civilian internees to places of safety immediately.

(4) His Majesty the Emperor has free to forbid their ultimate form of Government.

What Will Hirohito Do?

(From Our London Office)
LONDON, Aug. 13—Sir Robert Craigie, ex-British Ambassador, Tokyo, interviewed by the "Daily Express" answering question whether the Emperor can take orders from the Allied C-in-C. and still remain Emperor said, "Technically not, but as his country has been beaten he has no alternative to that and abdicating. My guess is that he will not abdicate but accept the situation to save his country further troubles and destruction." Sir Robert thought that there was every chance of Japan one day having a democratic government.

MIKADO NO FIGUREHEAD

WORLD'S MIGHTIEST MONARCH

One Of The Greatest Financial Power Of Japan

LONDON, Aug. 13.—The conception that the Mikado is but a figurehead is not borne out in fact. Politically and economically Emperor Hirohito holds greater powers than any monarch, but his religious authority is even greater far beyond any political and economic dictator through out the world.

Facts reveal that the Emperor is two of the greatest financial powers through out Japan and holds 141,000 shares of the Bank of Japan, shares of the Nippon Bank and contains but unquestionably large number of shares of the Yokohama Specie-Bank and Industrial Bank of Japan and 54,000 shares of the Mitsui-Bank, 181,000 shares of the famous Oba Paper Company, 20,000 shares of the South Manchurian railway, 24,000 shares of the Tokyo Electric Light company and 20,200 shares of the Taiwan Sugar Manufacturing Company.

Japanese Industrialists by making the Mikado a part of their economic oligarchy made him absolutely dominant in Japanese life. They, also believed that he was responsible for the surrender proposals also suggested that the retention of the Mikado's rule in Japan's post-war life, but their position is not different from that of German industrialists who during the last war took shelter behind the Kaiser and in this war behind Hitler.

What the Japanese Industrialists lost from foreign markets closing down after Pearl Harbour was made up from increased war business of heavy industries. The small businessmen who lost more from lack of foreign trade gladly accepted war orders as the Emperor together with his and small industrialists organised Japan's gigantic economic war machine all of whom there-after share Japan's war guilt and behind all this is the military clique and over all sits the Mikado.

Mikado Hirohito wielded such power that he could have kept Japan out of war. He presided over the Imperial Conference on July 2, 1941, where it was decided to conquer East Asia, even if it meant warring against the British Empire and the United States and it is believed that it was this conference where the attack on Pearl Harbour was planned.

IN FOOL'S PARADISE

Jap Consul In Eire Disbelieves Home Disasters

(From Our Special Correspondent)
DUBLIN, Aug. 13.—Setsuya Beppu, 45-year-old Japanese Consul-General at the most worried man. He with his young Japanese wife and Ichi Hachi, his consul, sits at the regency furnished drawing room in a suburban house sipping Indian tea and has not received mail and funds from Japan for some weeks. He reads the Irish and English newspapers, but does not believed them. "Most of these stories about devastating bomb raids are propaganda by the Americans for terrorist purposes." He says that if Japan is defeated he would like to settle in Eire and if he has any family he would like to send them to an Irish school.

SHE MARRIES 5 IN A WEEK

CAIRO, Aug. 13.—Police are still inquiring into the case of a young girl who, arrested after deserting a taxi driver 12 hours after they were wedded, actually was found to have married four other men the same week, all with the consent of her mother.—(C. P. of America.)

Printed & Published by BIJOLI KANTI GHOSH, for the PATRIKA PRESS, No. 13, Ananda Chatterjee Lane, and issued at the PATRIKA Post Office, CALCUTTA.

SIFTA SALT *for summer dishes*

Daily Mail
ADVANCE
FOR KING AND EMPIRE

Treat with care for extra wear
Bear Brand *Utility Stockings*

NO. 15,374   ONE PENNY   WEDNESDAY, AUGUST 15, 1945

Answer to atom bomb: *British scientists already at work* **See Page Two**

PEACE AT MIDNIGHT: JAPS SURRENDER

'Cease fire' order to Allies

'VJ'—TO-DAY AND TO-MORROW

JAPAN has surrendered unconditionally. This news was announced last night simultaneously in the four Allied capitals—London, Washington, Moscow, and Chungking. Allied forces have been ordered to "suspend offensive action."

Mr. Attlee announced the news to Britain in a broadcast at midnight and said that to-day and to-morrow would be VJ-Days. The King is to broadcast at 9 to-night. President Truman gave the news at a Press conference at the White House.

Japan's surrender—intimated in a code message of 160 words and sent through the Swiss Foreign Office at Berne last night—will be accepted by General MacArthur, as Supreme Allied Commander, as soon as arrangements are completed.

President Truman has ordered the Japanese Government to order the "Cease Fire" on all fronts and to send emissaries immediately to General MacArthur with information on the disposition of Japanese forces.

ACCEPTANCE IN FULL

Mr. Attlee, in his midnight broadcast, said : "Japan has to-day surrendered. The last of our enemies is laid low."

Then he read the Japanese reply.

" With reference to the announcement of August 10, regarding the acceptance of the provisions of the Potsdam Declaration and the reply of the Government of the United States, Great Britain, the Soviet Union and China sent by Secretary of State Byrnes on the date of August 11, the Japanese Government has the honour to reply to the Governments of the Four Powers as follows :

" **1.** His Majesty the Emperor has issued an Imperial Rescript regarding Japan's acceptance of the provisions of the Potsdam Declaration.

" **2.** His Majesty the Emperor is prepared to authorise and ensure the signature by his Government and the Imperial Headquarters of the necessary terms for carrying out the provisions of the Potsdam Declaration.

" **3.** His Majesty is also prepared to issue his commands to all military, naval, and air authorities to cease to all forces under their control wherever located to cease active resistance and to surrender arms and issue such other orders as may be required by the Supreme Commander of the Allied Forces for the execution of the above-mentioned terms."

VJ crowds march to West End at 3 a.m.

And New York lifts the roof

'At 3 a.m. to-day crowds which had celebrated all night in London's West End began to be reinforced by others from the East End. In donkey carts, lorries, and carts they arrived, while on prompt processions headed by bands swelled the throng. —Story in BACK PAGE.

From **DON IDDON,** Daily Mail Special Correspondent
New York, Tuesday.

WITHIN a few minutes of the announcement of the end of the war, New York was deluged with a storm of "ticker tape" and torn paper. Sirens hooted from ships in the harbour, crowds danced through the streets.

Americans abandoned all business and welcomed the end in a frenzy of emotion.

All day the streets of New York had been jammed with singing, shouting, horn-hooting, unruly crowds who waved flags, embraced strangers, mounted roofs of taxis and cars, hooted policemen on their shoulders and generally let the big blow off their pent-up feelings.

Rejoicing began early, when the announcement by Tokio radio that the Japanese had surrendered was flashed all over the country.

As soon as the first newspapers reached the streets the people were out in force, and the celebrations began.

WILDEST NIGHT

Times-square became the throbbing centre of the demonstration, in the biggest, wildest, and most tumultuous scene in the city's history.

The whole of upper Broadway was blocked with cheering, hilarious, exuberant crowds.

Paper had been fluttering down from skyscraper offices about early morning, and even bottles and whisky bottles were being hurled from windows by more aesthetic celebrants.

Police cars, fire engines, and riot squads had difficulty in handling the crowds along Broadway; police and military police and others patrolled from the U.S. Army service tried to help.

Some Service men were jostling civilians by light-heartedly firing their revolvers in the air and cutting of firecrackers and kissing screaming girls.

All over the town flag-decorated cars were sounding their horns abruptly and their radios were on at full blast.

WORK STOPS

Youths and girls were undo dancing in the squares and singing "God bless America" hoarse, immortal voices.

A good deal of drinking was going on, and New Year's Eve and election-night celebrations were pale and unvirile compared with the show that Manhattan will put on to-night.

The fact that the official announcement had yet to come was being ignored.

Many war fatalities and almost at offices, shops and stores were deserted. People in streets, on bars and in restaurants nearly everywhere, and raising merry hell. To-morrow the headlines will be swaggering.

TO-DAY

Call-up ends : More leave

By Daily Staff Reporter

CALLING-UP notices to the Forces and directions to munition examination will be suspended for seven days at noon to-day.

This "breathing space" may be extended at the end of the seven days.

No more directions to people to work in munition factories or in any factory or any production will be issued. People who have already received directions to report for war work, but have not yet done so, will have their direction notices withdrawn.

The Admiralty, War Office, and Air Ministry announced this morning :

"All personnel of Royal Navy, Army, and Royal Air Force now on leave (men while serving with the Forces and while on embarkation leave) and those on embarkation of Embarkation, leave, may add an additional 48 hours to their leave.

" This concession does not apply to those who are on leave from abroad whose cases to which they are due to return.

" Personnel on such leave, those on embarkation of whose on short-notice, or cancellations with previous instructions, on the date stated on their leave passes."

And the Japs wailed

New York, Tuesday.

THOUSANDS of Japanese outside the Imperial Palace, Tokio, to-day bowed their heads in misery and with tears running down their cheeks wailed : "Perhaps we are not enough?"

The public admission of shame is general, at the hands of the Allies being so widely publicised, and is expected to be provocative in the King's Speech by its appropriate.

The "Imperial decision " was not explained by the Japanese Press Agency which broadcast a long description of the weeping and wailing amid all emotion in the Far East.—Reuter.

875 lost in cruiser

Washington, Wednesday.

THE U.S. heavy cruiser Indianapolis has been lost, with 875 men missing.

Announcing this to-day, the Navy Department said she went down in the Philippine Sea from enemy action.

Every man of the 1,196 aboard was a casualty. The list is : Navy—five dead, 311 missing, 367 wounded ; Marine Corps — 26 missing, nine wounded.—Reuter.

New secretaries

The Foreign Secretary, Mr. Ernest Bevin, has appointed Mr. Pierson Dixon his Principal Private Secretary and Mr. Valentine Lawford Assistant Private Secretary.

MARSHAL AT MIDNIGHT MASS

Pétain to die: 'Guilty' verdict at 3 a.m.

JURY OUT SIX HOURS

From WALTER FARR, Daily Mail Special Correspondent
Paris, Wednesday Morning.

MARSHAL PÉTAIN was sentenced to death at 3 a.m. to-day after the jury had deliberated his fate for six hours.

The crowd outside the Palais de Justice waiting for the verdict became so large that the police decided to move them away from the building.

After midnight one of the strangest religious services ever held took place in the building.

To-day is the Feast of the Assumption and a national holiday in France. While Pétain and his wife were waiting to hear the verdict they requested that there might be a midnight Mass to celebrate the coming of the feast.

So 89-year-old Marshal, kneeling beside his wife, took part in this solemn religious service in a room surrounded by armed guards, while in another room 27 judges were deciding his fate.

Flushed, weary

Before he came from Pétain waited whether he had anything to say. Flushed and weary, he got slowly to his feet and read from a crumpled paper to about 1,000 firm : " I want to say to the French people ..."

"During this trial," he asserted, " I have kept deliberately silent ... having entrusted to the French people the reason for my attitude."

"My thought—my only thought—was to remain with the French people to the soil of France. ... I am innocent—I protest. ... I shall ..."

Poison fear

"Whatever happens now, the people of France will not forget. The people know that I defended them as I defended Verdun ..."

"Conscious of the suffering to my life and my liberty are to your hands, but my honour I entrust to my memory."

"After my long life, and having reached the threshold of ..."

BACK PAGE—Col THREE

Labour bid for 'new world' in policy

Higher wage riddle

By WILSON BROADBENT, Political Correspondent

PLANS for increasing the efficiency and productivity of British industry are being examined by the Labour Government.

Some indication of Mr. Attlee's intentions will be given—or implied—in the policy outlined in the speech which the King will deliver from the Throne in the House of Lords this morning.

Leading Labour Ministers realise that their political future depends on their approach to economics.

Mr. Attlee has devoted much of his long leisure, brooding, to the Government's policy.

Every effort

Every effort will be made to exert the early development of British industry.

Nationalisation of coal mines, and eventually of transport, is part of the Labour policy which has been widely publicised, and is expected to be announced in the King's Speech by its appropriate.

More coal

Yet Labour has promised to improve and increase the means and methods of distribution—a fundamental of Government policy—and this demands considerable concentration before it can be achieved.

The general impression is that Mr. Attlee's Government will not adopt any whole-sale schemes of nationalisation or any short cuts to the form of prosperity which it hopes to produce.

The shortest cut, will be the nationalisation of the Bank of England.

The nationalisation of mines, which may be delayed somewhat because the Labour Government is intent on increased production of coal at once, is one the lines of procedure.

Mr. Emanuel Shinwell, Minister of Fuel and Power, is preparing the necessary legislation.

Meanwhile he plans to legislate production for change, in the working conditions and the question of pay for miners.

'Quarry' boy is gaoled

For breaking out

A 14-YEARS-OLD boy was yesterday sent to prison for 14 days because there were no vacancies in an approved school. He was charged at Bradford Juvenile Court with absconding from Middlewood remand home. He was not defended.

Middlewood is the remand home at Bochdale where, a Home Office inspector has alleged, boys were forced to work in a quarry.

It was stated in court yesterday that the boy had broken out of the remand home several times.

The last time he was said to have escaped by breaking a window. Middlewood's new superintendent said he could not now be responsible for him.

Mr. Phillips, chairman of the court, remarked to the boy's father : "I'm afraid you've got a young scoundrel."

He was not being sent to prison because he was a scoundrel but because he had broken out.

Mr. Phillips said later that the Home Office had been informed and asked urgently to find room for him in an approved school.

"It is their responsibility now," he added.

Duke sees President

From Daily Mail Correspondent

Washington, Tuesday. — The Duke of Windsor to-day had a 35-minutes' talk with President Truman at the White House and also saw Mr. James F. Byrnes, Secretary of State.

U.S. PANDEMONIUM OF JOY

Washington, Tuesday.—There is a pandemonium of celebration to-night in Washington, New York, San Francisco.

The noise everywhere is deafening. Theatres and restaurants emptied at the news, and the jubilant crowds are singing, shrieking, and dancing in streets.

Many New York bars had to close their doors. Times-square is a solid mass of cheering people.—B.U.P.

A 5

PÉTAIN MAY GET MERCY

Paris radio states that the court expressed the wish, in view of Marshal Pétain's great age, death sentence should not be carried out. Pétain was thus condemned to maximum degradation and the application of his property.—Reuter and A.P.

PALACE CROWDS MASS AT 3 a.m.

Crowds began to mass outside Buckingham Palace just as the King's speech ended at the Palace as early as one o'clock.

Quite, Wednesday.—Admiral Mountz called off clock by noon to-day. British and U.S. war planes, when surrender flash received.—B.U.P.

B 5

WOMEN OFFER A HOME

To red tape 'orphans'

Hundreds of offers to provide homes for the poor "red tape orphans" of Dunkirk days have been pouring in to the N.S.P.C.C. from readers of the Daily Mail.

Edna aged seven, Margaret, aged six, Alice, aged three—these are youngsters twice been mentioned of neglecting their ...

Radar men may 'pick up' the moon

SIR ROBERT WATSON WATT
"father" of radar : His story is told on Page THREE.

SCIENTISTS in England are working on the location of nearer objects by radio reflections—and the possible radar location of the moon is being considered.

Mr Edward V. Appleton, secretary of the Department of Scientific and Industrial Research, told of this in a lecture to the Institution of Electrical Engineers.

Calculations showed, he said, that with a very powerful aeriel station and photo focusing at the receiving and receiving amongst an invisible wavelength the variable radio echoes after the radio waves have under their two-one-a-half second journey to the moon and back.

The distance away of a located object is found by timing the interval the radio wave is in the reflecting object and back—a distance which can be located at an interval of 160,000 miles a second.

Dr. E. V. Appleton himself—a young Cambridge don — and another Cambridge physicist, Mr. F Barnett, made the first experiments on the measurement of distance by radio reflections in 1925.

Their object was to prove the existence of the Heaviside layer and the measurement of its distance above the earth.

Radar secrets and pictures.—
Page THREE

FOOD *for* FACTS

making the MOST of CABBAGE

No one can afford to waste the food value of anything in these days of world shortage, certainly not mothers who want to see their families growing up strong and healthy. And because it's only too easy to waste the precious vitamins and minerals in green vegetables by incorrect cooking, these simple hints on preparing cabbage are well worth studying. It's easier at this time of year to follow the recommended health plan, "Eat a green, leafy vegetable at least once every day." Here's how to get the full benefit.

GOLDEN RULES FOR COOKING CABBAGE

To enjoy cabbage at its greenest, and full of delicious flavour, follow these rules. Prepare like this, it keeps most of its vitamins and mineral salts, and little of the food value is lost.

1. Use as fresh as possible. If you keep your garden, don't gather till wanted.

2. Allow ½ lb. for 4 portions. Remove faded, coarse outer leaves. Quarter the heart, cut up fine, removing the thicker stem ribs of the outside and central leaves and slice the rest. Wash rapidly, don't soak.

3. Use only the freshest, most thoroughly washed cooking whatever possible, and stalk and heart outside leaves.

4. Into boiling, salted water—about 1 in. deep in a fast-boiling pan—put cabbage gradually, so that boiling hardly stops.

5. Boil briskly for 10-15 minutes only. Shake pan occasionally.

6. Drain off any liquid. Use for gravy, etc.

7. Serve at once. Keeping hot or reheating destroys the vitamin C. Before serving add a teaspoon of margarine if possible, and toss well.

FOR VARIETY

All sorts of additions may be made to cabbage, or savory cooked in this way. A few chopped bacon rinds just before serving, and you have something extra new and interesting.

SUPPER SUGGESTION

Serve cabbage as a main dish, for supper or lunch, combined with cheese. For instance, try a saucepan filling of cooked cabbage, or perhaps a chunk of creamy sauce.

CABBAGE CREAMED through for the ingredients: ½ lb. shredded cabbage, ½ pint water, 1 level teaspoon salt, 2 tablespoons margarine, 2 level tablespoons of flour, ½ pint cabbage water, 2 tablespoons household milk, grated nutmeg and pepper. Method : boil half a pint water with salt, add the cabbage and cook till tender, 7 to 10 minutes. Strain and keep hot, reserve the cooking water, melt the fat and stir in the flour, add the cabbage water and milk, bring to a boil stirring well. Season. Serve hot. Suitable for ½ meals at supper.

SEE 9 WEEK 4 — THE LAST WEEK OF EATING FRESH No. 1 : SALT ½ Ref 79 OZ. 1840.
THE MINISTRY OF FOOD, LONDON, W.C.1

INDEX

Page numbers in italics refer to images and captions.

CREDITS

I am happy to acknowledge the extent to which this book has been a real team effort. The book's editor Gemma Maclagan has played a key part in getting the book together and keeping me on schedule.

Russell Knowles and Steve Behan are responsible for the book's strong visual content and layout.

Philip Parker and Terry Charman have between them made sure that the history is as error-free as it can be and I am grateful to them for their scrupulous monitoring of the text and captions which has made this a better book.

The majority of photographs reproduced in this book have been taken from the collections of the Photograph Archive at the Imperial War Museum. The reference numbers for each of the photographs are listed below, giving the page number, location and reference number.

Key: t = top, b = bottom, c = centre, l = left & r = right

7 t CAN 902, 7 b EA 38785, 8 NYF 9892, 12 NA 142, 13 NA 6630, 15 Department of Documents, 23 NYF 11281, 29 MH t 11250, 30-31 MH 1978, 32 NA 12810, 33 MH 1680, 35 HU 40203, 36-37 B 5114, 37 MH 10132, 38 t EA 26941, 38 b TR 2626, 39 Papers of the Rt Hon Viscount Montgomery of Alamein CMG CBE, 41 B 8441, 42 t FLA 5499, 42 b FRA 200371, 43 t 6781, 43 b HU 64137, 47 COL 34, 48 D 21313, 59 b B 9473, 61 t EA 34627, 61 b B 13169, 62 A 25247, 67 EA 37079, 70 HU 66477, 73 CL 1173, 74 t TR 174, 74 b HU 2126, 75 t HU 2129, 75 b E 16462, 81 H 6293, 82 HU 20288, 84-85 Department of Documents, 86 MH 12850, 88 EA 47958, 90 EA 48447, 111 t IA 13766, 111 b A 27813, 112 B 14413, 113 OWIL 64545, 116 t EQU 4088, 122-123 BU 4094, 124 BU 4269, 125 NYP 49945, 126 C 5149, 127 SE 3071, 128 SE 3773, 129 t SE 3006, 130 t IND 3143, 130 b SE 3891, 131 SE 3804, 132 NA 23837, 134 tl TR 2377, 134 b TR 2846, 135 HU 50242, 137 tr INS 8088, 139 HU 68178, 141 tr FIR 8573, 142 t FRA 203385, 145 Papers of the Rt Hon Viscount Montgomery of Alamein CMG CBE, 148-149 MH 29427, 151 HU 44878, 152 A 30427, 153 HU 53442

Photographs from sources from outside the Imperial War Museum:

Airbourne Museum 'Harenstein' Utrechtseweg 232, 6862 AZ Oosterbeek, Netherlands: 44-45

AKG-Images: 57, 59 t, 63, 68-69, 71 t, 137 tl, 137 b, 144, 146, 154

Australia War Memorial: 17 t 42999, 17 b REL34921, 18 t 127965, 18 b 16422, 19 70242, 20 l POO554_002,

Bastogne Historical Center, Colline du Mardasson, B-6600 Bastogne, Belgium: 90

BPK Bildagentur: 94

DPA: 89

Getty Images: AFP 120; /American Stock 106; /Bettmann 24, 83, 149, 155; /Corbis 9; /FOX Photos 105; /George W. Hales/Fox Photos 129 c; /Bernard Hoffman/The LIFE Picture Collection 104, 150; /Heinrich Hoffman/The LIFE Picture Collection 86 t; /Hulton Archive 93 b, 134 tr; /Keystone 70 t; /Keystone/Hulton Archive 64; /Popperfoto 65 t; /Paul Popper/Popperfoto via Getty Images 109; /Ivan Shagin 138-139; /Victor Temin/Slava Katamidze Collection 140-141; /Universal History Archive/UIG 147; /Roger Viollet 121 t

National Archives & Records Administration, Washington: 10-11, 25-27, 50, 51, 52, 53, 77 t, 77 b, 78, 79, 96, 98, 99, 100-103, 115, 116 b, 117, 118, 119, 156, 157

Photo12: Coll-DITE/USIS 65 b, 71 b; /Photosvintages 66

Shutterstock: AP 106-107, 108-109, 142b, 143

Topfoto: 14 b, 20-21, 54 l; /HIP 60; /Ullstein Bild 5, 14 t, 29 b, 49 l, 49 r, 54 r, 56-57, 93 t, 94-95, 113 c, 121 b

Every effort has been made to acknowledge correctly and contact the source and/or copyright holder of each picture and Welbeck Publishing apologises for any unintentional errors or omissions, which will be corrected in future editions of this book.